D0852246

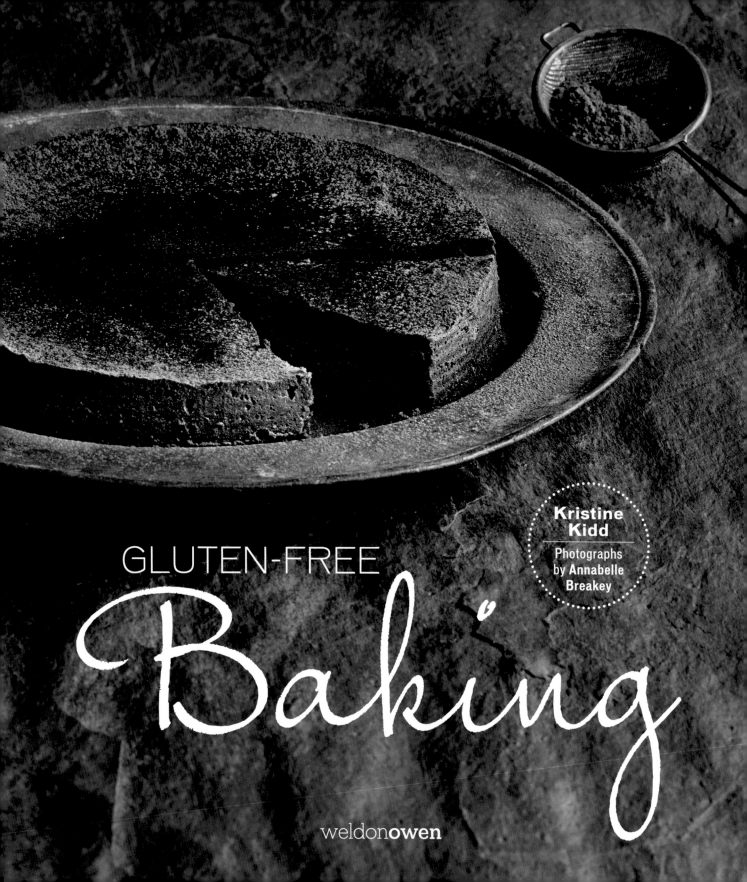

GLUTEN-FREE

Baking

Kristine Kidd

Photographs by Annabelle Breakey

weldon**owen**

GLUTEN-FREE GOODNESS......................6

INGREDIENT PRIMER......................9

TIPS & TRICKS......................12

morning treats......................15

cookies......................31

cakes......................51

pies & tarts......................65

puddings & custards..........79

other desserts......................93

breads......................107

A GLUTEN-FREE PANTRY......................122

BASIC RECIPES......................124

INDEX......................126

gluten-free goodness

For the first 2 years after I had to adopt a gluten-free diet, I gave up bread and many pastries because most of the prepared gluten-free goodies were coarse, dry, and lacking in good flavor. The flour blends were mixtures of nutritionally empty white starches, and I had no idea how to cook with whole grains like sorghum and buckwheat.

At first I relied on fresh fruit and ice cream sundaes for dessert. But after awhile, I wanted something more exciting for our dinner parties. So I started to focus on baked desserts that never included gluten—items like crisp meringue, Pavlovas topped with whipped cream and berries, nut tortes layered with lemon curd, and flourless chocolate cakes. Many of those recipes are in this collection.

When I began craving cookies and cakes, breads and pies, and breakfast pastries, I decided it was time to explore the alluring array of gluten-free whole grains I had been avoiding. I formulated the goal to create treats with great flavor and texture, featuring healthful grains, and as small a measure of white starches as I could get away with. I focused on slightly sweet, protein rich sorghum flour; earthy buckwheat flour; millet; oats; quinoa; and almond meal.

After much experimentation, I started producing satisfying breakfast pastries: flavorful scones with add-ins like chocolate chips, ginger, and lemon; fresh berry muffins; and my childhood favorite—cinnamon crumb cake.

Holidays were my next challenge. For the first few years I served apple crisp after our Thanksgiving feast, but last year I realized we all really missed pies. Nuts ground with gingersnaps make terrific crunchy crumb crusts, perfect for sweet spiced pumpkin pie. I am proud of the pie and tart crust I developed after many tests. Try it in the spectacular apple crumble pie, and I bet you'd never guess it was gluten-free. For Christmas, the intense, rich chocolate-cherry torte is an ideal ending. Or, how about a pumpkin cheesecake with a pecan crust?

When my stepson Ethan comes to visit, he heads straight for the kitchen and checks out the cookie tin for treats. These days I keep it filled with chocolate chip oatmeal cookies, rich walnut brownies, shortbread like pecan thumbprint cookies or his favorite, fudgy ginger-nut meringues.

Now I was on a roll, and began formulating delicacies for every occasion: creamy cheesecake with wild blueberry sauce for our anniversary, coconut-lime pie for my husband's birthday, gingerbread cake topped with sautéed peaches to end a summer garden party, and chocolate-nut-caramel tart for big deal dinners.

Finally, I was ready to tackle the artisanal breads I craved most of all, and what an adventure it has been! I didn't want to create disappointing copies of breads that rely on gluten for their structure and texture; I was determined to make great breads with the whole grains I was coming to love.

Cornbread came first— full flavored, whole-grain cornmeal supported with just enough starch to offer lift. I started with plain cornbread, and then moved onto versions with cheese and chilies or dried fruit and fennel seed. I discovered that Irish soda breads turned out great when made with subtly sweet oatmeal flour and wheat-like sorghum flour. I also make a multigrain, walnut enriched version as my everyday bread—great hot, toasted or plain, slathered with butter and jam or smeared with soft cheese.

I discovered that flat breads are pretty easy to re-create but high-rising loaves need gluten for support. I flavor my flatbreads with fresh herbs and olives and serve them with appetizers or alongside pasta dinners.

Dive into this book and before you know it, muffins, pies, cakes, cookies, and breads will be safely reintroduced back into your diet in new and—perhaps—even more delicious forms.

ingredient primer

Gluten is a protein present in wheat, rye, and barley. Most traditional baking recipes rely on the gluten present in wheat flour, and the development of its inherent proteins, for their structure. Gluten-free baking differs from traditional baking in that it uses non-gluten substitutes, different baking formulas, and unique baking solutions. Following is a guide to the main gluten-free ingredients used throughout this book.

Gluten-free flours and starches

BUCKWHEAT FLOUR

Made from ground buckwheat seeds, this flour has a strong, earthy flavor and dark color. I like to use it for breads, muffins, and scones.

CORNSTARCH

This highly refined starch has little nutritional value, but helps lend a smooth texture to gluten-free baked goods.

MILLET FLOUR

Dense in nutrients and mild in flavor, millet flour forms a pleasing, dense crumb. It works well in hearty breads.

OAT FLOUR

This subtly sweet, whole-grain flour is made from ground oats. Be sure to choose oat flour that is labeled as "gluten-free." Oat flour can easily be made at home in a food processor by grinding gluten-free oats until they become powdery. This flour is particularly high in protein, making it ideal for building structure in breads and muffins.

POTATO STARCH

This white starch, derived from potatoes, helps deliver tenderness and structure in baked goods, but it needs to be combined with other flours. Do not confuse it with potato flour, which is the whole vegetable—not just the starch— ground into flour.

QUINOA FLOUR

Made from pulverizing one of the most nutrient and protein dense grains available, quinoa flour is delicate and may retain a faint bitterness that is present in the whole grain. I use quinoa flour in my whole grain walnut bread.

RICE FLOUR

Brown rice flour is a sandy-textured flour that is slightly nutty and earthy, much like the flavor of brown rice in its whole form. Keep this flour in the refrigerator to extend its shelf life. More neutral in flavor and lighter in

Measuring flour

Baking recipes, whether traditional or gluten free, calls for careful and consistent measuring of ingredients in order to guarantee good results. For these recipes, I used the following technique for flour: Place the measuring cup on a sheet of waxed or parchment paper. Pour or spoon the flour into the cup (do not pack it down), and then level it off with a metal spatula or the back side of a knife; the overflow will fall onto the paper below. When you're finished measuring, lift up the paper from two sides, catching the overflow ingredients in the center, and then pour the excess flour back into its original container. For flour measured by tablespoons, scoop the flour into the measuring spoon and then level with the back of a knife.

Gluten-free flours and starches (continued)

color than brown rice flour, white rice flour has a longer shelf life. Although I don't use white rice flour for baking, it is great for thickening gravies and dusting meats before sautéing.

SORGHUM FLOUR

One of my favorite gluten-free ingredients, sorghum flour is high in protein and fiber, and adds a pleasant smooth texture to baked goods. I use it in everything from muffins and scones to piecrusts and quick breads. Many believe sorghum flour to be closest in flavor and texture to wheat flour.

TAPIOCA FLOUR

Also known as tapioca starch, this fine powder helps contribute texture and structure to baked goods. Tapioca flour should always be mixed with other gluten-free flours for best results.

Whole grains, flakes, and meals

ALMOND MEAL/FLOUR

Made from blanched or unblanched ground almonds, almond meal, also called almond flour, contributes a subtle nutty and sweet flavor to recipes. You can make your own by grinding almonds in a food processor until they produce a fine, flour-like

texture. Overgrinding will result in nut butter. Almond meal is one of my favorite ingredients for muffins, scones, cakes, crusts, and crumb toppings, thanks to its flavor and rustic texture.

CORNMEAL

Not all cornmeal is created equal. Be sure to look for whole grain yellow cornmeal. I like Bob's Red Mill, because it is full flavored and medium grind, which is perfect for muffins, breads, and fruit crisps.

FLAXSEED MEAL

Nutty and high in protein, flaxseed meal provides nutrients and structure to baked goods. It is high in omega-3 fatty acids. I like to use flaxseed meal to add texture and flavor to breads.

OATS

Not all oats or oat products are guaranteed to be free of gluten, as they are sometimes processed in facilities where they may come in contact with wheat or may be contaminated during growing and shipping. Be sure that the oat product states that it is gluten free on the label. Many of my recipes call for rolled oats, which are whole oat groats that have been steamed, pressed, and dried. Minimally processed, rolled oats are still considered a whole-grain product. I use them for muffins, cookies, and fruit crisps.

OAT BRAN

Oat bran adds texture and fiber to baked goods, lending a pleasing, rustic texture to bread.

QUINOA FLAKES

I recently discovered quinoa flakes, and use them as an alternative to oats in crisps. They are made by rolling whole grains of quinoa into thin flakes. Quinoa flakes can also be used for a quick, hot, high-protein cereal.

Mix-and-match flours

As you've just read, there are a wide range of flours that can be used in gluten-free baking, and many of them are interchangeable. When you are making substitutions, keep in mind that it's best to substitute flours that have a similar texture. For example, medium-textured flours such as sorghum, oat, and brown rice flours can generally be substituted for one another. Heavy-textured flours and meals, like buckwheat, chickpea, millet, quinoa, cornmeal, and nut meals are typically interchangeable.

Baking oils

For the recipes in this book, feel free to use whatever type of baking oil you prefer, but it's a good idea to choose one that has a neutral or complementary flavor to other ingredients in the recipe. My favorite is mild

tasting extra-virgin olive oil for its healthful qualities. But other good suggestions are almond, avocado, canola, coconut (melted before using), corn, peanut, safflower, and sunflower oil.

Dairy and dairy alternatives

Many of my recipes call for dairy products—milk, cream, eggs, and the like. That said, it can be common for those with a gluten sensitivity or intolerance to find that they have a similar intolerance to dairy products. Many of the recipes inside this book offer substitutions for using nondairy milks, such as soy milk. I found that by cutting out dairy for a period of time, and then gradually adding it back to my diet, I was able to tolerate dairy products again.

Xanthan gum

Xanthan gum is a plant-based ingredient that adds structure and elasticity to baked goods. Many gluten-free flour blends include xanthan gum in the mix, but the recipes in this book use homemade flour combinations, and therefore sometimes require the addition of a little xanthan gum in order to achieve a texture and structure similar to that created by using gluten.

Safeguarding against cross-contamination

If not everyone in your family is gluten free, you'll want to protect yourself or loved ones from accidental gluten contamination. First, set aside a dedicated cupboard in which only gluten-free products are stored. Reserve one or more cutting boards exclusively for non-gluten food prep (even a crumb from wheat bread can compromise the immune system of someone with a gluten sensitivity or allergy). Finally, depending on how severe the gluten sensitivity is in your household, you may wish to purchase a separate set of tools and equipment to help avoid contact with ingredients that contain gluten. Color code the handles of the utensils that you use for gluten-free cooking. Consider a toaster, colanders, and other kitchen supplies and utensils, including sponges and dish towels in severe cases.

tips & tricks

The ingredients used in gluten-free baking behave a bit differently than those in standard baking recipes. Here are a few things I learned when developing the recipes for this book.

GENERAL TIPS

• Because gluten-free muffins are very tender, I like to line the muffin cups with paper liners. Buttering the muffin cups works well, too, just be careful not to break the muffins when you unmold them.

• Scones made with gluten-free flour are very delicate, so I like to cut them into shapes after baking to ensure they hold together.

• When using almond meal, be sure to break up any clumps before measuring, and whisk the batter well to blend the almond meal evenly with the other ingredients.

• When substituting nuts in my recipes, be sure to weigh the appropriate amount, rather than measure them by volume. Differently shaped nuts will yield different volumes, and will affect the recipe results.

• When making gluten-free piecrust, you don't need to take as much care with the dough as with wheat-based piecrust, as there is no gluten present that can be overworked. However, to ensure that the desired flaky texture is achieved, take care that all of the ingredients are cold, as you would with traditional pastry dough.

• I shop for spices—cinnamon, cardamom, fennel seeds, and more—at an Indian market a few times a year. They have a great selection, and cost a fraction of supermarket spices. I buy big bags and then share them with friends.

• Many of my recipes call for a mixture of milk and vinegar which adds tenderness. If you like, you can substitute the same volume of buttermilk.

WORKING WITH EGG WHITES

• For best results, use older eggs (save the fresh-from-the-farm eggs for your breakfast).

• Eggs are easiest to separate when cold, but they whip better when they are at room temperature. After separating, let the egg whites stand for about 15 minutes to warm them to room temperature

• Separate egg whites into a small bowl one at a time and remove any broken yolk or shells.

• When whipping egg whites, be sure to select a clean, dry, and grease-free bowl. Even a speck of grease can hinder whipping.

• When making meringue, measure all the ingredients before starting to whip the whites.

• When whipping egg whites into meringue, add the sugar gradually while beating constantly; this helps produce maximum volume and a smooth texture

• Use meringue batter right after it reaches the proper consistency, then bake as soon as it is formed into the desired shape on the baking sheet. Be sure your oven is fully preheated before preparing meringues.

• When making custards, such as the pots de crème on page 83, save the egg whites for making meringues. The whites will keep, covered, in the refrigerator for 2–4 days, or they can be frozen for up to 12 months.

morning treats

Cinnamon Crumb Cake......**18**

Raspberry
Oatmeal Muffins.................**21**

Almond–Sour
Cherry Muffins..................**22**

Cornmeal-Pecan
Muffins **23**

Gingerbread
Blackberry Muffins.............**24**

Rosemary-Buckwheat
Scones...........................**27**

Lemon-Blueberry Scones...**28**

Chocolate Chip-Ginger
Scones...........................**29**

The approach I took

to develop gluten-free versions of breakfast favorites involved making use of naturally gluten-free products whenever possible. I had mixed results when I used gluten-free flour blends that I bought at the store, so I opted to create customized mixtures of gluten-free flours, depending on what type of baked good I was making. While the process was a bit daunting at first, once I set up a solid gluten-free baking pantry (see my tips on page 122), I had everything I needed on hand in my kitchen. The recipes took a lot of trial and error to perfect, but I hope you'll enjoy the fruits of my labor in your own kitchen. The effort was well worth the delicious results!

Start your morning with gluten-free delights

Muffins, scones, and coffee cakes are popular at the breakfast table, but it can be hard to find quality, gluten-free items in the bakery or supermarket. Enter these delicious treats, which I developed to satisfy my love for iconic morning delicacies, and customized for a gluten-free lifestyle. Sorghum flour and almond meal are two of my staple ingredients, because I enjoy the rustic flavor and texture they each contribute. Many of these treats can be frozen for unexpected overnight guests or brunch entertaining (no one will guess they are gluten free). In addition to what you see here, there are other great breakfast recipes throughout this book, including many of the breads on pages 107–121 and the quiches on pages 73 and 75.

MOIST, TENDER CRUMB CAKE topped with crunchy cinnamon streusel was one of the treats I missed most when I went gluten-free. I am very proud of the cake I developed, and my friends who stopped by my house while I was working on the book can't wait to have the recipe so that they can make it too.

cinnamon crumb cake

FOR THE CAKE

1½ cups (7 oz/160 g) sorghum flour

1 cup (7 oz/220 g) firmly packed brown sugar

½ cup (1½ oz/45 g) almond meal

½ cup (2½ oz/75 g) potato starch

2 teaspoons ground cinnamon

1½ teaspoons xanthan gum

1¼ teaspoons baking powder

1 teaspoon baking soda

¾ teaspoon kosher salt

1 cup (8 oz/250 g) plain yogurt

3 large eggs

½ cup (4 fl oz/125 ml) oil or melted butter

1 tablespoon pure vanilla extract

FOR THE TOPPING

½ cup (1¾ oz/55 g) sorghum flour

½ cup (3½ oz/105 g) firmly packed brown sugar

½ cup (2 oz/60 g) walnut pieces, toasted

1 teaspoon ground cinnamon

¼ teaspoon kosher salt

¼ cup (2 oz/60 g) cold unsalted butter, cut into ½-inch (12-mm) pieces

serves 8–12

1 To make the cake, preheat the oven to 350°F (180°C). Line a 9-inch (23-cm) square baking pan with parchment paper.

2 In a large bowl, whisk together the sorghum flour, brown sugar, almond meal, potato starch, cinnamon, xanthan gum, baking powder, baking soda, and salt. In a bowl, whisk together the yogurt, eggs, oil, and vanilla. Add the liquid ingredients to the dry ingredients and stir until smooth. Scrape the batter into the prepared pan.

3 To make the topping, in a food processor, pulse the sorghum flour, brown sugar, walnuts, cinnamon and salt until blended.

Add the butter and pulse until the mixture begins to form clumps. Spoon the topping evenly over the batter.

4 Bake the cake until springy to the touch and a toothpick inserted into the center comes out clean, about 45 minutes. Let cool on a wire rack for at least 40 minutes. Cut into squares or rectangles. Serve warm or at room temperature.

✳ I've made this cake with millet flour in place of the almond meal, and it is almost as good. Replace the walnuts in the topping with pecans, almonds, or hazelnuts, if you like. The cinnamon could be replaced with a mixture of half cardamom, half cinnamon, or add a touch of cardamom and/or nutmeg for an exotic flavor.

CHEWY, TOASTED OATS in the batter make these muffins moist and tender. I love the surprise of breaking open a muffin and discovering plump, bright pink raspberries inside. I like to sprinkle these with a crunchy nut topping, but they are also delicious without. I find it works best to line the cups with papers.

raspberry oatmeal muffins

FOR THE MUFFINS

¾ cup (2½ oz/75 g) gluten-free rolled oats

½ cup (2¾ oz/80 g) gluten-free oat flour

½ cup (1½ oz/45 g) almond meal

½ cup (1¾ oz/55 g) sorghum flour

1 teaspoon baking powder

¾ teaspoon baking soda

½ teaspoon *each* xanthan gum, kosher salt, and ground cardamom

¾ cup (6 fl oz/180 ml) plus 3 tablespoons whole milk or soy milk

1 tablespoon distilled white vinegar

⅔ cup (5 oz/155 g) firmly packed dark or golden brown sugar

¼ cup (2 fl oz/60 ml) oil or melted butter

2 large eggs

1 teaspoon pure vanilla extract

1 cup (4 oz/125 g) raspberries

FOR THE TOPPING

¼ cup (1 oz/30 g) walnut pieces

¼ cup (¾ oz/20 g) gluten-free rolled oats

3 tablespoons firmly packed dark or golden brown sugar

⅛ teaspoon ground cardamom

2 tablespoons cold unsalted butter, cut into ¼-inch (6-mm) pieces

makes 12 muffins

1 Preheat the oven to 325°F (165°C). Line 12 standard muffin cups with paper liners or grease the cups with butter or cooking spray.

2 To make the muffins, spread the rolled oats on a small baking sheet. Bake until starting to brown, about 10 minutes. Transfer to a large bowl and let cool completely. Once cool, add the oat flour, almond meal, sorghum flour, baking powder, baking soda, xanthan gum, salt, and cardamom and whisk to blend.

3 In a glass measuring cup, combine the milk and vinegar. Let stand until thickened, about 5 minutes.

4 Raise the oven temperature to 425°F (220°C). In a bowl, whisk together the milk mixture, the brown sugar, oil, eggs, and vanilla. Add the liquid ingredients to the dry ingredients and stir until combined. Let stand for 15 minutes.

5 Meanwhile, make the topping. In a food processor, pulse the walnuts, oats, brown sugar, and cardamom until the nuts are coarsely chopped. Add the butter and pulse until the mixture resembles a fine meal.

6 Stir the raspberries into the batter. Spoon the batter into each muffin cup, filling it almost to the top. Sprinkle about 1 tablespoon of the topping evenly over each.

7 Place the pan in the oven and immediately reduce the temperature to 375°F (190°C). Bake the muffins until springy to the touch and a toothpick inserted into the center comes out clean, about 25 minutes. Let the muffins cool in the pan on a wire rack for 10 minutes, then transfer them to a wire rack to cool completely. Serve warm or at room temperature. Store in an airtight container at room temperature for up to 2 days.

RICH IN ALMOND MEAL, these muffins are tender and sophisticated, like mini nut cakes. Butter enhances the cakelike quality, but oil can be used instead. Add ⅓ cup (2 oz/60 g) mini chocolate chips or chopped semisweet chocolate for an elegant variation.

almond–sour cherry muffins

¾ cup (6 fl oz/180 ml) plus 3 tablespoons whole milk or soy milk

1 tablespoon distilled white vinegar

2 large eggs

6 tablespoons (3 oz/90 g) unsalted butter, melted, or oil

1 teaspoon almond extract

½ teaspoon pure vanilla extract

1 cup (3½ oz/105 g) sorghum flour

¾ cup (6 oz/185 g) firmly packed brown sugar

⅔ cup (2 oz/60 g) almond meal

⅓ cup (1¾ oz/50 g) potato starch or ⅓ cup (1¼ oz/35 g) tapioca flour

1 teaspoon baking powder

¾ teaspoon baking soda

½ teaspoon ground cinnamon

½ teaspoon kosher salt

½ teaspoon xanthan gum

1 cup (6 oz/185 g) dried sour cherries

¼ cup (1 oz/30 g) sliced almonds

makes 12 muffins

1 Preheat the oven to 375°F (190°C). Line 12 standard muffin cups with paper liners.

2 In a glass measuring cup, combine the milk and vinegar. Let stand until thickened, about 5 minutes. Add the eggs, melted butter, almond extract, and vanilla and whisk until blended. In a bowl, whisk together the sorghum flour, brown sugar, almond meal, potato starch, baking powder, baking soda, cinnamon, salt, and xanthan gum. Add the liquid ingredients to the dry ingredients and whisk until smooth. Let stand for 10 minutes.

3 Stir the cherries into the batter. Spoon the batter into each muffin cup, filling it almost to the top. Sprinkle the sliced almonds evenly over each, dividing them evenly.

4 Bake the muffins until springy to the touch and a toothpick inserted into the center comes out clean, about 20 minutes. Let the muffins cool in the pan on a wire rack for 10 minutes, then transfer them to a wire rack to cool completely. Serve warm or at room temperature. Store in an airtight container at room temperature for up to 2 days.

✳ When using almond flour, be certain to break up any clumps before measuring, and use a whisk to blend the almond meal evenly with the other ingredients in the batter.

I LOVE BAKING with whole-grain, gluten-free cornmeal. It adds tenderness, good flavor, and enough structure that little additional starch is needed. Cinnamon and pecans turn a simple corn bread batter into delightful breakfast muffins.

cornmeal-pecan muffins

FOR THE MUFFINS

¾ cup (6 fl oz/180 ml) plus 3 tablespoons whole milk or soy milk

1 tablespoon white vinegar

2 large eggs

¼ cup (2 fl oz/60 ml) oil or melted butter

¾ teaspoon grated orange zest

1 cup (4½ oz/14 g) gluten-free whole-grain cornmeal

⅔ cup (5 oz/155 g) firmly packed brown sugar

½ cup (1¾ oz/55 g) sorghum flour

½ cup (2½ oz/75 g) potato starch

1 teaspoon baking powder

¾ teaspoon *each* baking soda and ground cinnamon

½ teaspoon *each* kosher salt and xanthan gum

1 cup (4 oz/125 g) coarsely chopped pecans, lightly toasted

FOR THE TOPPING

¼ cup (1 oz/30 g) pecans

¼ cup (¾ oz/20 g) gluten-free rolled oats

3 tablespoons firmly packed brown sugar

⅛ teaspoon ground cinnamon

2 tablespoons cold unsalted butter, cut into ¼-inch (6-mm) pieces

makes 12 muffins

1 Preheat the oven to 350°F (180°C). Line 12 standard muffin cups with paper liners.

2 To make the muffins, in a glass measuring cup, combine the milk and vinegar. Let stand until thickened, about 5 minutes. Add the eggs, oil, and orange zest and whisk with a fork until blended.

3 In a bowl, whisk together the cornmeal, brown sugar, sorghum flour, potato starch, baking powder, baking soda, cinnamon, salt, and xanthan gum. Add the liquid ingredients to the dry ingredients and stir until combined. Let stand for 10 minutes.

4 Meanwhile, make the topping. In a food processor, pulse the pecans, oats, brown sugar, and cinnamon until the pecans are coarsely chopped. Add the butter and pulse until the mixture resembles a fine meal.

5 Stir the 1 cup pecans into the batter. Spoon the batter into each muffin cup, filling it almost to the top. Sprinkle 1 tablespoon of the topping evenly over each.

6 Bake the muffins until springy to the touch and a toothpick inserted into the center comes out clean, about 20 minutes. Let the muffins cool in the pan on a wire rack for 10 minutes, then transfer them to a wire rack to cool completely. Serve warm or at room temperature. Store in an airtight container at room temperature for up to 2 days.

✻ I like to bake these with olive oil because it's healthful, but choose one with a delicate flavor. Any baking oil you like or melted butter will work well. Brown sugar adds a rich flavor to baked goods along with sweetness. Be sure to use potato starch and not potato flour.

MY HUSBAND LOVES these for a quick breakfast with his morning coffee. I learned about how to use buckwheat in baked goods at a gluten-free retreat I attended. It adds nutrients, earthy flavor, and good structure to these muffins and other treats.

gingerbread blackberry muffins

FOR THE MUFFINS

¾ cup (6 fl oz/180 ml) plus 3 tablespoons whole milk or soy milk

1 tablespoon white vinegar

2 large eggs

¼ cup (2 fl oz/60 ml) oil or melted butter

2 tablespoons dark molasses

1⅓ cups (4½ oz/140 g) sorghum flour

⅔ cup (5 oz/155 g) firmly packed brown sugar

⅓ cup (2 oz/60 g) almond meal

3 tablespoons *each* buckwheat flour and potato starch

1 teaspoon baking powder

¾ teaspoon baking soda

¾ teaspoon *each* ground ginger, cinnamon, and allspice

½ teaspoon *each* kosher salt and xanthan gum

1¼ cups (6 oz/185 g) fresh blackberries

FOR THE TOPPING

½ cup (2½ oz/75 g) toasted hazelnuts or whole almonds

3 tablespoons firmly packed brown sugar

⅛ teaspoon ground ginger

2 tablespoons cold unsalted butter, cut into ¼-inch (6-mm) pieces

makes 12 muffins

1 Preheat the oven to 350°F (180°C). Line 12 standard muffin cups with paper liners.

2 To make the muffins, in a glass measuring cup, combine the milk and vinegar. Let stand until thickened, about 5 minutes. Add the eggs, oil, and molasses and whisk until blended. In a bowl, whisk together the sorghum flour, brown sugar, almond flour, buckwheat flour, potato starch, baking powder, baking soda, ginger, cinnamon, allspice, salt, and xanthan gum. Add the liquid ingredients to the dry ingredients and stir until combined. Let stand for 10 minutes.

3 To make the topping, in a food processor, pulse the hazelnuts, brown sugar, and ginger until the hazelnuts are coarsely chopped. Add the butter and pulse until the mixture resembles a fine meal.

4 Stir the blackberries into the batter. Spoon the batter into each muffin cup, filling it almost to the top. Sprinkle about 1 tablespoon of the topping evenly over each.

5 Bake the muffins until springy to the touch and a toothpick inserted into the center comes out clean, about 20 minutes. Let the muffins cool in the pan on a wire rack for 10 minutes, then transfer them to a wire rack to cool completely. Serve warm or at room temperature. Store in an airtight container at room temperature for up to 2 days.

✳ Pecans would also be a good choice for the topping. If the blackberries are large, cut them in half.

FRESH ROSEMARY, coarsely ground black pepper, extra-virgin olive oil, and earthy buckwheat combine to make a hearty, savory accompaniment to eggs or other breakfast dishes. All scones are best the day they are made, but these will keep in an airtight container for up to 3 days. Reheat them in a 300°F (150°C) oven for about 8 minutes.

rosemary–buckwheat scones

Extra-virgin olive oil for brushing

1 cup (3½ oz/105 g) sorghum flour

⅓ cup (2 oz/60 g) potato starch or ⅓ cup (1¼ oz/35 g) tapioca flour or ⅓ cup (1½ oz/45 g) cornstarch

¼ cup (1 oz/30 g) buckwheat flour

3 tablespoons firmly packed brown sugar

2 tablespoons almond meal

1 tablespoon minced fresh rosemary, plus 1 teaspoon minced rosemary for the topping

1½ teaspoons baking powder

1 teaspoon xanthan gum

¾ teaspoon baking soda

½ teaspoon kosher salt, plus more for sprinkling

½ teaspoon freshly ground black pepper, plus more for sprinkling

6 tablespoons (3 oz/90 g) cold unsalted butter, cut into ½-inch (12-mm) pieces

⅔ cup (2½ oz/75 g) plain low-fat yogurt

1 large egg

makes 8–10 scones

1 Preheat the oven to 375°F (190°C). Brush a 9-inch (23-cm) metal pie pan with olive oil.

2 In a food processor, pulse the sorghum flour, potato starch, buckwheat flour, brown sugar, almond meal, the 1 tablespoon rosemary, baking powder, xanthan gum, baking soda, ½ teaspoon salt, and ½ teaspoon pepper until evenly combined. Add the butter and pulse until the mixture resembles coarse meal, about 20 times. In a small bowl, whisk together the yogurt and egg with a fork until blended. Add the yogurt mixture to the food processor and process until a rough batter forms, about 10 seconds.

3 Scrape the batter into the prepared pan, spreading evenly. Brush the surface of the batter with olive oil. Sprinkle the top of the batter with the 1 teaspoon rosemary and a light sprinkle of salt and pepper.

4 Bake the scone until brown and springy to the touch, about 30 minutes. Transfer the pan to a cooling rack. Cut the scone into 8–10 wedges. Let cool at least 15 minutes. Serve warm or at room temperature. Store in an airtight container at room temperature for up to 3 days or freeze for up to 2 weeks.

 Add chopped Kalamata olives to give these scones a distinct Mediterranean flavor. Using yogurt helps tenderize the batter.

WHOLE-GRAIN SCONES are a favorite on Sunday mornings or when a friend is coming over for afternoon tea. Richly flavored, I don't usually offer butter with them, but preserves are a good addition. They are best when freshly baked, but can also be rewarmed in a 300°F (150°C) oven for about 8 minutes.

lemon-blueberry scones

1 cup (3½ oz/105 g) sorghum flour

⅓ cup (2 oz/60 g) potato starch or
⅓ cup (1¼ oz/35 g) tapioca flour or
⅓ cup (1½ oz/45 g) cornstarch

¼ cup (2 oz/60 g) firmly packed brown sugar

3 tablespoons buckwheat flour

3 tablespoons almond meal

1½ teaspoons baking powder

1 teaspoon xanthan gum

¾ teaspoon baking soda

½ teaspoon kosher salt

6 tablespoons (3 oz/90 g) cold unsalted butter, cut into ½-inch (12-mm) pieces

⅔ cup (2½ oz/75 g) plain nonfat or low-fat yogurt

1 large egg

2 teaspoon grated lemon zest

1 teaspoon pure vanilla extract

½ cup (3 oz/90 g) dried wild blueberries

2 tablespoons whole milk

1 tablespoon granulated sugar

⅛ teaspoon ground nutmeg

makes 8–10 scones

1 Preheat the oven to 375°F (190°C). Butter a 9-inch (23-cm) metal pie pan.

2 In a food processor, pulse the sorghum flour, potato starch, brown sugar, buckwheat flour, almond meal, baking powder, xanthan gum, baking soda, and salt until evenly combined. Add the butter and pulse until the mixture resembles coarse meal, about 20 times. In a small bowl, whisk together the yogurt, egg, lemon zest, and vanilla with a fork until blended. Add the yogurt mixture to the food processor and process until a rough batter forms, about 10 seconds. Add the blueberries and pulse once to mix in.

3 Scrape the batter into the prepared pan, spreading evenly. Brush the surface of the batter with the milk. In a small bowl, stir together the granulated sugar and nutmeg and sprinkle evenly over the batter.

4 Bake the scone until brown and springy to the touch, about 30 minutes. Transfer the pan to a cooling rack. Cut the cake into 8–10 wedges. Let cool at least 15 minutes. Store in an airtight container at room temperature for up to 3 days or freeze for up to 2 weeks. Serve warm or at room temperature.

❋ This is a basic recipe, so add any flavorings and additions that inspire you—raisins, dried cranberries, nuts, and chocolate chips can all replace the blueberries. Ground cinnamon or ginger can replace the nutmeg.

CHOCOLATE CHIPS, crystallized ginger, and almond meal transform a simple scone batter into something perfect for a special occasion. I created these luxurious morning treats for a girlfriend's birthday brunch and no one even realized they were gluten-free.

chocolate chip–ginger scones

1 cup (3½ oz/105 g) sorghum flour

6 tablespoons (1¼ oz/35 g) almond meal

⅓ cup (2 oz/60 g) potato starch or ⅓ cup (1¼ oz/35 g) tapioca flour or ⅓ cup (1½ oz/45 g) cornstarch

¼ cup (2 oz/60 g) firmly packed brown sugar

1½ teaspoons baking powder

1 teaspoon xanthan gum

¾ teaspoon baking soda

½ teaspoon plus ⅛ teaspoon ground cinnamon

½ teaspoon kosher salt

6 tablespoons (3 oz/90 g) cold unsalted butter, cut into ½-inch (12-mm) pieces

⅔ cup (2½ oz/75 g) plain nonfat or low-fat yogurt

1 large egg

½ teaspoon pure vanilla extract

½ cup (3 oz/90 g) mini chocolate chips

⅓ cup (2 oz/60 g) finely chopped crystallized ginger

1 tablespoon unsalted butter, melted

1 tablespoon granulated sugar

makes 8–10 scones

1 Preheat the oven to 375°F (190°C). Butter a 9-inch (23-cm) metal pie pan.

2 In a food processor, pulse the sorghum flour, almond meal, potato starch, brown sugar, baking powder, xanthan gum, baking soda, ½ teaspoon cinnamon, and salt until evenly combined. Add the butter and pulse until the mixture resembles coarse meal, about 20 times. In a small bowl, whisk together the yogurt, egg, and vanilla with a fork to until blended. Add the yogurt mixture to the food processor and process until a rough batter forms, about 10 seconds. Add the chocolate chips and ginger and pulse to mix in.

3 Scrape the batter into the prepared pan, spreading evenly. Brush the surface of the batter with the melted butter. In a small bowl, stir together the granulated sugar and the ⅛ teaspoon cinnamon and sprinkle evenly over the batter.

4 Bake the scone until brown and springy to the touch, about 30 minutes. Transfer the pan to a cooling rack. Cut the cake into 8–10 wedges. Let cool at least 15 minutes. Store in an airtight container at room temperature for up to 3 days or freeze for up to 2 weeks. Serve warm or at room temperature

✱ Because my scones are delicate, I bake them in a pie pan, which helps hold their shape. Unlike scones made from wheat flour, these are cut into individual scones after baking.

cookies

Fudgy Ginger-Nut
Meringues...........................**34**

Chocolate Chip
Oatmeal Cookies................**37**

Vanilla Spice Meringues.....**38**

Chocolate-Chip
Meringues...........................**39**

Chocolate Walnut
Brownies............................**40**

Coconut Macaroons...........**43**

Pine Nut &
Almond Cookies.................**44**

Almond-Ginger Crisps.......**45**

Almond-Oat
Lace Cookies......................**47**

Pecan Thumbprint
Cookies..............................**48**

I've always loved meringues, even before I switched to a gluten-free lifestyle. Today, they anchor my dessert repertoire, and I have developed many variations of meringue-based cookies and desserts that I adore. Admittedly, I miss many of the cookies and brownies from my childhood that remind me of happy times, so I have created gluten-free versions of my favorite recipes. I'm really excited to share them with you here. The secret to success is to use a combination of different flours and flavorings—especially nuts and nut flours—to create the deep flavors that I crave in cookies and bars without sacrificing texture or richness.

Stock your cookie jar with new classic treats

Cookies and bars are indulgences beloved by everyone and I enjoy having them on hand when guests drop by. There are dozens of variations on the following pages, so you'll be able to customize many of the recipes to your own taste and have endless alternatives for your cookie jar. For example, the oatmeal cookies on page 37 can be made either relatively healthy or indulgent, depending on what you mix in; the pecan thumbprint dough on page 48 can be shaped into three entirely different cookies; and the brownies on page 40 can be flavored in myriad ways. If you are making meringues, be sure to read the troubleshooting tips on page 12 before you start. If it is a humid day, opt for one of the other recipes instead.

CRISP ON THE OUTSIDE, gooey on the inside, and with a surprising hit of ginger, these cookies keep well in a cookie tin if they don't get gobbled up the day they are baked. These embellished meringues are naturally gluten free.

fudgy ginger-nut meringues

4 oz (125 g) bittersweet chocolate, chopped

2 large egg whites, at room temperature

⅛ teaspoon cream of tartar

½ cup (4 oz/125 g) sugar

½ teaspoon pure vanilla extract

⅛ teaspoon kosher salt

¾ cup (3½ oz/105 g) hazelnuts, toasted and coarsely chopped

⅓ cup (2 oz/60 g) finely chopped crystallized ginger

makes about 20 cookies

1 Preheat the oven to 325°F (165°C). Line a large baking sheet with parchment paper.

2 In the top of a double boiler set over (not touching) simmering water, place the chocolate. Stir until melted and smooth. Remove from over the water and let cool slightly.

3 In a stand mixer, beat the egg whites on medium speed until frothy, about 2 minutes. Add the cream of tartar and beat on medium-high speed until soft peaks form, about 2 minutes. Gradually add the sugar, 1 tablespoon at a time, beating until the whites are stiff, about 3 minutes. Beat in the vanilla and salt just until incorporated. Using a rubber spatula, gently fold in the hazelnuts and ginger, followed by the melted chocolate, leaving some white streaks of egg white for a marbled appearance.

4 Dab a bit of the batter underneath the corners of the parchment paper to secure it to the baking sheet. Immediately drop the batter by rounded tablespoons onto the prepared baking sheet, spacing them about 1 inch (2.5 cm) apart.

5 Bake the cookies until dry and crisp on the outside but still soft inside, about 10 minutes. Let the cookies cool on the baking sheet on a wire rack for 10 minutes, then gently transfer them to wire racks to cool completely. Store in an airtight container at room temperature for up to 5 days.

✱ Feel free to play around with the flavors, replacing the hazelnuts with toasted pecans, walnuts, almonds, or toasted coconut. Be sure to measure the nuts and ginger before you start beating the egg whites so they are ready to go before the meringue is whipped.

CHEWY, YET LIGHT, filled with oats and chocolate chips, and not too sweet, these are addictive oatmeal cookies. Think of the dough as a basic formula for your own variations—swap in dried fruit and/or nuts for the chocolate chips. For my wedding rehearsal dinner, I mixed in ½ cup (3 oz/90 g) finely chopped crystallized ginger and 1 cup (6 oz/185 g) dried sour cherries, and everyone asked for the recipe.

chocolate chip oatmeal cookies

1 cup (3½ oz/105 g) sorghum flour

¼ cup (2¾ oz/80 g) gluten-free oat flour

½ cup (3½ oz/105 g) tapioca flour or ½ cup (2½ oz/75 g) potato starch

1 teaspoon xanthan gum

1 teaspoon baking powder

¾ teaspoon kosher salt

½ teaspoon baking soda

½ teaspoon ground cinnamon

½ teaspoon ground cardamom

¼ teaspoon ground allspice

¾ cup (6 oz/185 g) unsalted butter, at room temperature

1½ cups (10½ oz/330 g) firmly packed brown sugar

2 large eggs

2 teaspoons pure vanilla extract

2½ cups (7½ oz/235 g) gluten-free rolled oats

1 cup (6 oz/185 g) chocolate chips, or dried fruit, or 1 cup (4–5 oz/125–155 g) nuts

makes about 3 dozen cookies

1 Place racks in the upper and lower thirds of the oven and preheat to 325°F (165°C). Line 2 large baking sheets with parchment paper.

2 In a bowl, whisk together the sorghum flour, oat flour, tapioca flour, xanthan gum, baking powder, salt, baking soda, cinnamon, cardamom, and allspice.

3 In the bowl of a stand mixer fitted with the paddle attachment, beat the butter on medium speed, until light, about 2 minutes. Add the brown sugar and beat until light and fluffy, about 2 minutes. Add the eggs, 1 at a time, beating until each one is incorporated. Beat in the vanilla just until incorporated. Add the dry ingredients and beat on medium speed just until blended. Add the rolled oats and chocolate chips and mix until incorporated. Let the dough stand for 10 minutes.

4 With dampened hands, shape the dough into 1½-inch (4-cm) balls. Place the cookies on the prepared baking sheets, spacing them about 2 inches (5 cm) apart.

5 For chewy cookies, bake until golden and still slightly soft in the center, about 12 minutes. For crisp cookies, bake until golden and just firm in the center, about 14 minutes. Let the cookies cool on the baking sheets on wire racks for 3 minutes, then transfer them to wire racks to cool completely. Store in an airtight container at room temperature for up to 5 days, or freeze for up to 1 month.

✳ The cardamom in the recipe lends irresistible flavor and fragrance, but if you don't have any, increase the cinnamon to 1 teaspoon and you won't be disappointed.

DELICATE TREATS with a tantalizing surprise, these lighter-than-air meringue cookies are flavored with cinnamon, cardamom, and allspice. Whenever I serve a fruit dessert, I pile a plate high with these and put them at the center of the table.

vanilla spice meringues

8 tablespoons (4 oz/125 g) sugar

⅛ teaspoon ground cinnamon

⅛ teaspoon ground cardamom

⅛ teaspoon ground allspice

2 large egg whites, at room temperature

¼ teaspoon cream of tartar

1 teaspoon pure vanilla extract

⅛ teaspoon kosher salt

makes about 2 dozen meringues

1 Place racks in the upper and lower thirds of the oven and preheat the oven to 200°F (95°C). Line 2 baking sheets with parchment paper.

2 In a bowl, mix 2 tablespoons of the sugar with the cinnamon, cardamom, and allspice.

3 In a stand mixer, beat the egg whites on medium speed until frothy, about 2 minutes. Add the cream of tartar and beat on medium-high speed until soft peaks form, about 2 minutes. Gradually add the remaining 6 tablespoons (3 oz/90 g) of the sugar, 1 tablespoon at a time, beating until the whites are stiff, about 3 minutes. Beat in the vanilla and salt just until incorporated. Add the spiced sugar mixture to the meringue and continue to beat until very stiff, glossy, and the meringue holds a peak when the beater is lifted straight up, about 2 minutes longer.

4 Dab a bit of the meringue underneath the corners of the parchment papers to secure them to the baking sheets. Immediately drop the meringue by rounded tablespoons onto the prepared baking sheets, scraping off the meringue with another spoon and spacing them about 1½ inches (4 cm) apart.

5 Bake the meringues until dry, crisp, and firm, 1½–2 hours, switching the baking sheets halfway though. Turn off the oven, open the door, and let the cookies cool in the oven 10 minutes. Transfer to wire racks and let cool completely on the baking sheets. Store in an airtight container at room temperature for up to 5 days.

✳ For extra goodness, fold 1 cup (5 oz/155 g) chopped toasted hazelnuts or almonds into the batter just before forming the cookies.

BAKE A BATCH of these chocolatey treats, fragrant with a touch of cinnamon, and your kitchen will smell divine. These are great served on their own, with a cup of coffee or tea, or alongside a bowl of ice cream or sorbet.

chocolate-chip meringues

8 tablespoons (4 oz/125 g) sugar

¼ teaspoon ground cinnamon

2 large egg whites, at room temperature

¼ teaspoon cream of tartar

1 teaspoon pure vanilla extract

⅛ teaspoon kosher salt

1 cup (6 oz/185 g) mini chocolate chips or chopped bittersweet or semisweet chocolate

makes about 32 meringues

1 Place racks in the upper and lower thirds of the oven and preheat the oven to 200°F (95°C). Line 2 baking sheets with parchment paper.

2 In a bowl, mix 2 tablespoons of the sugar with the cinnamon.

3 In a stand mixer, beat the egg whites on medium speed until frothy, about 2 minutes. Add the cream of tartar and beat on medium-high speed until soft peaks form, about 2 minutes. Gradually add the remaining 6 tablespoons (3 oz/90 g) of the sugar, 1 tablespoon at a time, beating until the whites are stiff, about 3 minutes. Beat in the vanilla and salt just until incorporated. Add the cinnamon-sugar mixture to the meringue and continue beating until very stiff, glossy, and the meringue holds a peak when the beater is lifted straight up, about 2 minutes longer. Using a rubber spatula, gently fold in the chocolate chips.

4 Dab a bit of the meringue underneath the corners of the parchment papers to secure them to the baking sheets. Immediately drop the meringue by rounded tablespoons onto the prepared baking sheets, scraping off the meringue with another spoon and spacing them about 1½ inches (4 cm) apart.

5 Bake the cookies until dry, crisp, and firm, 1½–2 hours, switching the baking sheets halfway though. Turn off the oven, open the door, and let the cookies cool in the oven 10 minutes. Transfer to wire racks and let cool completely on the baking sheets. Store in an airtight container at room temperature for up to 5 days.

✳ For a nutty meringue, replace the chocolate chips with 1 cup (4–5 oz/125–155 g) chopped nuts—toasted almonds, walnuts, pecans, or toasted hazelnuts are all good choices.

DEEP, DARK, FUDGY BROWNIES, these have an intense chocolate flavor from both chocolate and cocoa powder. Cocoa powder provides most of the structure for these brownies, with just a little sorghum and tapioca flour to hold them together. I like to use bittersweet chocolate, but if you prefer a slightly sweeter brownie, use semisweet chocolate instead. It is important to beat the batter for at least 1 minute; otherwise the brownies will be very crumbly.

chocolate walnut brownies

8 oz (250 g) bittersweet or semisweet chocolate, chopped

6 tablespoons (3 oz/90 g) unsalted butter, cut into pieces

¾ cup (6 oz/185 g) firmly packed brown sugar

2 large eggs

1 teaspoon pure vanilla extract

2 tablespoons unsweetened cocoa powder

1 tablespoons sorghum flour

1 tablespoon tapioca flour or potato starch

⅛ teaspoon kosher salt

1 cup (4 oz/125 g) walnuts, toasted and coarsely chopped

makes 1 dozen brownies

1 Preheat the oven to 350°F (180°C). Line an 8-inch (20-cm) square baking pan with foil, letting some excess foil extend up 2 opposite sides of the pan. Butter the foil.

2 In a saucepan over low heat, melt the chocolate and butter until smooth, stirring constantly. Remove the pan from the heat, add the brown sugar, and stir well. Stir in the eggs, 1 at a time, then stir in the vanilla. Add the cocoa powder, sorghum flour, tapioca flour, and salt and whisk vigorously until the batter is silky and no longer grainy, at least 1 minute. Stir in the walnuts. Scrape the batter into the prepared pan.

3 Bake until the brownies are just set in the center and a toothpick inserted into the center comes out with moist crumbs, 25–30 minutes. Let the brownies cool completely in the pan on a wire rack.

4 Holding the ends of the foil, lift the brownies onto a cutting surface. Peel back the foil sides. Using a large, sharp knife, cut into 12 rectangles. Store at room temperature, covered with foil, for up to 3 days, or freeze for up to 1 month.

✳ Pecans or toasted hazelnuts are good alternatives to the walnuts. For cappuccino brownies, add 1½ teaspoons of instant coffee powder and ½ teaspoon ground cinnamon. For mint brownies, leave out the nuts and add 1½ teaspoons peppermint extract. For orange-nut brownies, substitute toasted hazelnuts for the walnuts and add 1 tablespoon grated orange zest.

THESE HEAVENLY MACAROONS have the perfect texture—crunchy on the outside, chewy on the inside. I can't decide if I like them better dipped in chocolate or plain, so I usually dip only half of the cookies and offer them both ways.

coconut macaroons

¼ cup (2 oz/60 g) unsalted butter, at room temperature

Pinch of kosher salt

6 tablespoons (3 oz/90 g) sugar

¼ teaspoon pure vanilla extract

¼ teaspoon almond extract

1 egg plus 1 egg white, at room temperature

12 oz (375 g) sweetened flaked coconut (3 firmly packed cups)

4 oz (125 g) bittersweet or semisweet chocolate, chopped (optional)

makes about 2 dozen cookies

1 Preheat the oven to 325°F (165°C). Line 2 large rimmed baking sheets with parchment paper.

2 In a bowl of a stand mixer fitted with the paddle attachment, beat the butter and salt until smooth, about 2 minutes. Add the sugar and beat until well blended, about 2 minutes. Beat in the vanilla and almond extracts just until incorporated. Beat in the egg and then the egg white, beating until each one is incorporated. Mix in the coconut.

3 Drop the batter by rounded tablespoons onto the prepared baking sheets, spacing them about 1½ inches (4 cm) apart and mounding them slightly with the spoon. Using damp fingers, gently press any loose coconut into the mounds.

4 Bake the macaroons, 1 sheet at a time, until golden brown, about 20 minutes. Let the cookies cool completely on the baking sheets on wire racks.

5 To dip the macaroons in chocolate, if desired, line a baking sheet with waxed paper. Place the chocolate in the top of a double boiler over barely simmering water. Heat, stirring often, until melted and smooth. Remove from over the water and set aside to cool slightly. One at a time, dip the bottom of each macaroon in the melted chocolate. Place the macaroon, chocolate side down, on the waxed paper. Repeat with the remaining macaroons. Refrigerate until the chocolate is set, about 45 minutes.

6 Store the undipped macaroons in an airtight container at room temperature up to 5 days. Store the chocolate-dipped macaroons in an airtight container in the refrigerator.

✳ These freeze well for up to 1 month, so keep a batch in the freezer for unexpected guests.

THESE SWEET DELICACIES rely on ground nuts for their crisp texture. For the last several years, my husband has been asking me to re-create the biscuit-like pine nut cookies he loves from the south of France. He says I got them right with this recipe.

pine nut & almond cookies

2 cups (10 oz/315 g) pine nuts

1½ cups (7 oz/220 g) slivered blanched almonds, toasted

⅔ cup (5 oz/155 g) sugar

2 large egg whites, at room temperature

¼ teaspoon kosher salt

⅛ teaspoon almond extract

makes about 2½ dozen cookies

1 Place racks in the upper and lower thirds of the oven and preheat to 325°F (165°C). Line 2 large baking sheets with parchment paper.

2 In a food processor, process 1 cup (5 oz/155 g) of the pine nuts, the almonds, and ⅓ cup (2½ oz/80 g) of the sugar until finely ground.

3 In a stand mixer on high speed, beat the egg whites, salt, and almond extract until soft peaks form, about 2 minutes. Reduce the speed to medium and gradually add remaining ⅓ cup (2½ oz/80 g) sugar 1 tablespoon at a time, beating just until incorporated. Increase the speed to high and continue beating until the whites are very stiff, glossy, and hold a peak when the beater is lifted

straight up, about 4 minutes longer. Using a rubber spatula, gently fold in the ground nut mixture.

4 Drop the batter by rounded tablespoons onto the prepared baking sheets, spacing them 2 inches (5 cm) apart. With dampened hands, shape the cookies into rounds or ovals and flatten slightly. Top each cookie with the remaining 1 cup pine nuts, dividing evenly.

5 Bake the cookies until golden, about 20 minutes, switching the baking sheets halfway through. Let the cookies cool on the baking sheets on wire racks for 5 minutes, then transfer them to wire racks to cool completely. Store in an airtight container at room temperature for up to 5 days.

✱ These have a distinctive pine nut flavor. However, you can vary the proportion of pine nuts to almonds in the batter to your taste; just be sure to use a total of 17 oz (530 g) nuts. Lightly butter the baking sheets to help anchor the parchment paper before forming the cookies. See the tips on page 12 for working with egg whites.

WONDERFULLY CRISP, and very easy to make, these almond-ginger cookies use almond butter to provide both the fat and substance of the batter, so no flour or butter is needed. These are perfect for a snack or alongside ice cream, sorbet, or fruit desserts.

almond-ginger crisps

1 cup (10 oz/315 g) smooth almond butter, well stirred

¾ cup (6 oz/185 g) firmly packed brown sugar

⅓ cup (2 oz/60 g) finely chopped crystallized ginger

1 large egg

1 teaspoon baking soda

1 teaspoon pure vanilla extract

⅛ teaspoon kosher salt

makes about 20 cookies

1 Preheat the oven to 325°F (165°C).

2 In a bowl, combine the almond butter, brown sugar, ginger, egg, baking soda, vanilla, and salt. Using a wooden spoon, stir vigorously until the dough is smooth and thick. Drop the dough by rounded tablespoons onto a large, ungreased baking sheet, spacing them about 1½ inches (4 cm) apart.

3 Bake the cookies until they puff, and then settle down, and they feel just set when gently touched, about 15 minutes. Let the cookies cool on the baking sheet on a wire rack for 5 minutes, then transfer them to a wire rack to cool completely. Store in an airtight container at room temperature for up to 5 days.

✱ Replace the almond butter with peanut butter for a tasty variation. I also like these without the ginger, and sometimes mix in mini chocolate chips.

THIN AND FRAGILE, and scented with orange zest, these delicate cookies are perfect with a cup of tea. They taste of caramelized sugar with a hint of orange. They are also delicious made with pecans or hazelnuts in place of the almonds. For nut-free cookies, substitute an equal quantity of oats.

almond-oat lace cookies

6 tablespoons (1 oz/30 g) gluten-free rolled oats

¼ cup (1½ oz/45 g) whole unblanched almonds

6 tablespoons (3 oz/90 g) unsalted butter

⅓ cup (3 oz/90 g) granulated sugar

⅓ cup (2½ oz/75 g) firmly packed brown sugar

1 tablespoon tapioca flour

1½ teaspoons grated orange zest

¾ teaspoon pure vanilla extract

¼ teaspoon kosher salt

makes about 2 dozen cookies

1 Preheat the oven to 350°F (180°C). Line 2 baking sheets with parchment paper.

2 In a food processor, pulse the oats and almonds until the mixture resembles coarse meal, about 15 times. In a heavy-bottomed saucepan over medium heat, melt the butter. Add the granulated and brown sugars and cook, stirring constantly, until the sugars dissolve. Remove the pan from the heat. Stir in the oat-almond mixture, the tapioca flour, orange zest, vanilla, and salt.

3 Spoon the batter by scant 1-tablespoon portions onto the prepared baking sheets, spacing them about 2½ inches (6 cm) apart and stirring the batter frequently to recombine. With dampened hands, press the cookies into disks that are ¼-inch (6-mm) high, smoothing out any jagged edges.

4 Bake the cookies, 1 sheet at a time, until dark golden brown and spread into thin rounds, about 10 minutes. Slide the sheets of parchment onto wire racks to let the cookies cool completely. Store in an airtight container at room temperature for up to 5 days.

✱ These cookies spread a lot while baking, so be certain to space them at least 2½ inches (6 cm) apart. For a variation, using a small spoon or fork, drizzle melted chocolate (bittersweet, semisweet, or milk chocolate are all delicious) on the surface of the baked, cooled cookies. Refrigerate the cookies until the chocolate is set. Store in the refrigerator in an airtight container for up to 5 days.

MY GRANDMOTHER taught me to make thumb-print cookies when I was just six years old. This recipe is based on my memory of those treats, modified for my gluten-free lifestyle. But I still fill half the cookies with jam and half with cinnamon sugar, just as my grandmother did.

pecan thumbprint cookies

FOR THE DOUGH

1½ cups (6 oz/185 g) pecan pieces

½ cup (4 oz/125 g) sugar

½ cup (4 oz/125 g) brown rice flour

½ cup (2 oz/60 g) cornstarch

1½ teaspoons grated lemon zest

¼ teaspoon kosher salt

½ cup (4 oz/125 g) cold unsalted butter, cut into ½-inch (12-mm) pieces

½ teaspoon pure vanilla extract

1 large egg yolk

FOR THE FILLING

¼ cup (2 oz/60 g) sugar mixed with ¾ teaspoon ground cinnamon (optional)

Rasperry or blackperry preserves, or your favorite jam (optional)

*makes about
2½ dozen cookies*

1 In a food processor, pulse 1 cup (4 oz/125 g) of the pecans and the sugar until the pecans are finely ground. Add the rice flour, cornstarch, lemon zest, and salt and pulse to mix well. Add the butter and vanilla and pulse until the mixture resembles a fine meal. Add the remaining ½ cup (2 oz/60 g) pecans and pulse once to mix in. Add the egg yolk and pulse until the dough starts to form a ball. Transfer the dough to a bowl and refrigerate until firm, about 30 minutes.

2 Place racks in the upper and lower thirds of the oven and preheat the oven to 325°F (165°C). Line 2 baking sheets with parchment paper.

3 With dampened hands, shape the dough into 1-inch (2.5-cm) balls. Place the balls on the prepared baking sheets, spacing them about 1½ inches (4 cm) apart. With your fingertip, make a well about ¼ inch (6 mm) deep in the center of each ball. Fill the well with cinnamon sugar or jam, or fill half the cookies with cinnamon sugar and half the cookies with jam. Refrigerate the cookies on the baking sheets for 10 minutes.

4 Bake the cookies until they start to color and the bottom edges are light brown, about 15 minutes. Let the cookies cool on the baking sheet on a wire rack for 2 minutes, then gently transfer them to wire racks to cool completely. Store the cookies in an airtight container at room temperature for up to 5 days.

✳ The pecans can be replaced with toasted walnuts, hazelnuts, or almonds. To make pecan shortbread cookies, form the dough into balls and flatten them slightly, but don't make a thumbprint. For Mexican wedding cookies, form the dough into balls but do not flatten them; once the cookies have baked and cooled, roll them in confectioners' sugar to coat.

cakes

Cheesecake with
Blueberry Sauce 54

Lemon Curd
Almond Cake 56

Chocolate-Cherry
Torte 59

Blackberry
Cornmeal Cake 60

Pumpkin-Spice
Cheesecake 61

Gingerbread &
Sautéed Peaches 63

For special occasions, there are few things as fitting as a cake—from elaborate tortes and luxurious cheesecakes for big events to simple, rustic creations for brunches, casual gatherings, and family events. To develop the tempting gluten-free gems on the pages that follow, I started with easy-to-adapt cheesecakes. Since the cream-cheese filling is naturally free of gluten, the cheesecakes just needed an updated crust made with ground nuts or crushed gluten-free cookies. Some of the other cakes took a little more experimentation to get right, as I needed to find the best combination of gluten-free flours, nuts, and eggs. Once you try the tempting cakes on the pages that follow, I hope you'll agree that I got these right.

End a special-occasion meal with a special cake

Everyone loves a homemade cake and I love to bake them, especially for special celebrations or when I'm entertaining. I developed these half-dozen cakes so that they would be approachable enough for a busy home cook to make, but indulgent enough to impress friends or family at a party. Many of the following cakes can be made ahead of time, allowing you to attend to other parts of the meal just before the guests arrive. Like the baked goods throughout this book, these recipes rely on a mixture of different gluten-free flours for their texture and structure. These recipes, in particular, use a small amount of tapioca starch, potato starch, or cornstarch to lend a lightness and softness to the crumb.

THE WILD BLUEBERRY SAUCE that tops this rich cheesecake reminds me of living in Vermont, where I'd pick the berries in a nearby forest. Here, a traditional cream cheese filling is lightened with ricotta and flavored with vanilla and lemon. The crust is a simple mixture of ground hazelnuts, sugar, and butter.

cheesecake with blueberry sauce

FOR THE CRUST

2 cups (10 oz/315 g) hazelnuts, toasted

¼ cup (2 oz/60 g) sugar

Pinch of kosher salt

¼ cup (2 oz/60 g) unsalted butter, melted

FOR THE FILLING

2 packages (8 oz/250 g each) cream cheese, cut into cubes, at room temperature

2 cups (1 lb/500 g) good-quality whole-milk ricotta cheese

¾ cup (6 oz/185 g) sugar

1 tablespoon plus 1 teaspoon grated lemon zest

2 teaspoons cornstarch

2 teaspoons pure vanilla extract

¼ teaspoon kosher salt

⅓ cup (3 fl oz/80 ml) heavy cream

5 large eggs, at room temperature

Wild Blueberry Sauce (page 124)

serves 12

1 Preheat the oven to 325°F (165°C). Line the bottom of a 9-inch (23-cm) springform pan with a round of parchment paper. Wrap the outside of the pan tightly with 3 layers of heavy-duty foil, covering the bottom and sides completely.

2 To make the crust, in a food processor, pulse the nuts, sugar, and salt until finely ground. Add the butter and pulse until moist clumps form. Scrape the mixture into the prepared pan and press evenly into the bottom and about 1¼ inches (3 cm) up the sides. Refrigerate until firm, about 20 minutes.

3 To make the filling, wipe out the food processor bowl and, process the cream cheese until smooth. Add the ricotta and process until mixed. Add the sugar, lemon zest, cornstarch, vanilla, and salt and process until mixed. Add the cream and process until evenly mixed. Add the eggs 1 at a time,

processing until each is mixed. Scrape the filling into the crust-lined pan and jiggle to even out the top.

4 Bring a kettle of water to a boil. Place the cake pan into a large roasting pan and add enough hot water to the roasting pan to come halfway up the sides of the cake pan. Bake the cheesecake until the edges are set and the center jiggles when the springform pan is gently shaken, about 1 hour 20 minutes. Carefully remove the springform pan from the roasting pan and then remove the foil. Transfer to a wire rack to cool completely in the pan, about 1 hour. Cover and refrigerate the cake, uncovered, overnight.

5 Using a small, sharp knife, cut around the cake's edges to loosen. Remove the pan sides. Transfer the cake to a platter. Cut the cake into wedges, spoon some sauce over the top, and serve.

✳ If you prefer to use fresh ricotta, spoon the cheese into a fine-mesh sieve lined with coffee filters set over a bowl and let drain in the refrigerator for at least 4 hours.

TANGY LEMON CURD and whipped cream make a luxurious filling and topping for this delicate cake. Fresh berries or thin lemon slices are pretty garnishes.

lemon curd almond cake

Butter for the pans
2¼ cups (7 oz/200 g) almond meal
¾ teaspoon baking soda
½ teaspoon ground cinnamon
6 large eggs, separated
⅔ cup (5 oz/155 g) sugar
2 tablespoons grated lemon zest
2 tablespoons fresh lemon juice
½ teaspoon kosher salt
¼ teaspoon cream of tartar
Lemon Curd and Whipped Lemon Frosting (page 124)

serves 8

1 Preheat the oven to 350°F (180°C). Butter two 8-inch (20-cm) cake pans. Line the bottoms with parchment rounds and butter the parchment. In a bowl, combine the almond meal, baking soda, and cinnamon. In a large bowl, whisk together the egg yolks, ⅓ cup (2½ oz/80 g) of the sugar, the lemon zest, and lemon juice until smooth.

2 In a stand mixer, beat the egg whites on medium speed until frothy, about 2 minutes. Add the salt and cream of tartar and beat on medium-high speed until soft peaks form, about 2 minutes. Gradually add remaining ⅓ cup (2½ oz/80 g) sugar, 1 tablespoon at a time, beating until stiff peaks form.

3 Add the almond mixture to the egg yolk mixture, stirring with a wooden spoon. Fold in one-third of the beaten egg whites to lighten the batter. Then, in 2 additions, gently fold in the remaining whites just until incorporated. Spoon the batter into the prepared pans, dividing it evenly.

4 Bake the cakes until brown, springy to the touch, and a tester inserted into the center comes out clean, about 25 minutes. Transfer the cakes to wire racks. Using a small, sharp knife, cut around the cakes' edges to loosen. Let cool completely in the pans.

5 Make the curd and frosting as directed.

6 To assemble the cake, put 1 cooled cake layer, rounded side up, on a platter. Using an offset or rubber spatula, evenly spread half of the reserved lemon curd on top of the cake. Spread about one-quarter of the frosting over the curd. Top with the second cake layer, rounded side up. Evenly spread the top of the cake with the remaining curd, then spread the remaining frosting over the top and sides of the cake. Place a few toothpicks in the top of the cake, and cover with plastic wrap. Refrigerate until ready to serve, up to 1 day.

✽ For a casual look, leave the sides unfrosted. Spread all of the lemon curd on top of the first cake layer and add a few big spoonfuls of whipped frosting. Frost the top of the cake with billows of the whipped frosting.

INDULGENT AND RICH, I created this cake for my stepson's birthday, and it's worthy of a special occasion. Definitely for chocolate lovers, it is dark, intensely chocolaty, and rich. The cake keeps well in the refrigerator, so it can be baked ahead of time.

chocolate-cherry torte

1 cup (6 oz/185 g) dried sour cherries such as Montmorency

3 tablespoons aged balsamic vinegar, cassis, rum, or brandy

1 cup (4½ oz/140 g) slivered blanched almonds, toasted

4 tablespoons (2 oz/60 g) granulated sugar

12 oz (375 g) bittersweet (60%) chocolate, chopped, or bittersweet chocolate chips such as Ghirardelli

¾ cup (6 oz/185 g) unsalted butter, cut into cubes

6 large eggs

1 cup (7 oz/220 g) firmly packed brown sugar

¼ teaspoon kosher salt

Unsweetened cocoa powder for dusting

Whipped Cream (page 124)

serves 12

1 In a small bowl, combine the cherries and vinegar and let soak for 2 hours.

2 Preheat the oven to 350°F (180°C). Butter a 9-inch (23-cm) springform pan and line the bottom with a round of parchment paper. Wrap the outside of the pan tightly with 3 layers of heavy-duty aluminum foil, covering the bottom and sides completely.

3 In a food processor, pulse the almonds until finely chopped. Add 2 tablespoons of the granulated sugar and pulse until the almonds are finely ground (do not overprocess).

4 In the top of a double boiler set over (not touching) simmering water, combine the chocolate and butter. Heat, stirring often, until the chocolate and butter are melted and smooth. Remove the bowl from over the water.

5 In a large bowl, whisk together the eggs and brown sugar until well blended. Gradually add the chocolate mixture, whisking until smooth. Stir in the ground almond mixture and salt, and then the

cherry mixture. Scrape the batter into the prepared pan and jiggle to even out the top of the filling.

6 Bring a kettle of water to a boil. Place the cake pan in a large roasting pan and add enough hot water to the roasting pan to come halfway up the sides of the cake pan. Cover the cake pan with aluminum foil but do not fold down the edges.

7 Bake the cake until set in the center and the outer 1 inch (2.5 cm) is dry to the touch (the top will be shiny), about 1 hour 40 minutes. Carefully remove the cake pan from the roasting pan and then the foil from the cake pan. Transfer the cake to a wire rack to cool completely in the cake pan, about 2 hours. Cover and refrigerate the cake until chilled, at least 3 hours and up to 3 days.

8 To serve, remove the sides of the pan and transfer the cake to a platter. Dust the cake with cocoa powder. Cut the cake into thin wedges and dollop with whipped cream. Serve chilled or at room temperature.

THIS RUSTIC DESSERT was inspired by the luscious ricotta and fruit cakes served at Huckleberry Bakery & Café in Santa Monica, one of my favorite places for brunch. It's like a cross between a moist cake and a cobbler. It's delicious on its own, but can also be topped with dollops of whipped cream or yogurt mixed with a little sugar.

blackberry cornmeal cake

1 cup (3¾ oz/120 g) gluten-free whole-grain cornmeal such as Bob's Red Mill

1½ teaspoons baking powder

1 teaspoon baking soda

½ teaspoon kosher salt

½ cup (4 oz/125 g) unsalted butter, at room temperature

¾ cup (6 oz/185 g) granulated sugar

2 large eggs

1 cup (3 oz/90 g) almond meal

½ cup (4 oz/125 g) whole-milk ricotta cheese

½ cup (4 oz/125 g) plain yogurt

1 tablespoon grated lemon zest

1 teaspoon pure vanilla extract

2 cups (8 oz/250 g) fresh blackberries

2 tablespoons firmly packed brown sugar

serves 8

1 Preheat the oven to 350°F (180°C). Butter a 9-inch (23-cm) springform pan and line the bottom with a round of parchment paper.

2 In a bowl, whisk together the cornmeal, baking powder, baking soda, and salt. Using a mixer on medium speed, beat the butter until light and creamy, about 2 minutes. Add the granulated sugar and beat until fluffy about 2 minutes. Add the eggs, 1 at a time, beating until each one is incorporated. Add the almond meal, ricotta, yogurt, lemon zest, and vanilla and beat until blended. Fold in the cornmeal mixture.

3 Scrape the batter into the prepared pan. Scatter the blackberries on top and sprinkle with brown sugar.

4 Bake the cake until brown, springy to the touch, and a tester inserted into the center comes out clean, about 1 hour. Transfer the cake to a wire rack. Using a small, sharp knife, cut around the cake's edges to loosen. Let cool completely in the pan.

5 To serve, remove the sides of the pan and transfer it to a platter. Cut the cake into wedges. Serve at room temperature.

✻ If you like, substitute blueberries for the blackberries. Leftovers keep well for about 3 days.

LUXURIOUSLY CREAMY, this rich cheesecake makes the flavors of pumpkin and spice shine through. It was inspired by my friend Karen—one of the best home bakers I know—and it's a variation on a cake she once brought to a holiday party. The crumb crust is made with ground pecans and easy-to-find gluten-free gingersnaps.

pumpkin-spice cheesecake

FOR THE CRUST

1 cup (4 oz/125 g) pecan pieces

1 cup (4 oz/125 g) gluten-free gingersnap crumbs

2 tablespoons firmly packed brown sugar

5 tablespoons (2½ oz/75 g) unsalted butter, melted

FOR THE FILLING

2 packages (8 oz/250 g each) cream cheese, cut into cubes, at room temperature

¾ cup (6 oz/185 g) firmly packed brown sugar

5 large eggs, at room temperature

⅓ cup (3 fl oz/80 ml) heavy cream

2 tablespoons cornstarch

¾ teaspoon pure vanilla extract

1 teaspoon ground cinnamon

¼ teaspoon ground ginger

¼ teaspoon ground nutmeg

¼ teaspoon kosher salt

1 can (15 oz/470 g) pumpkin purée

Candied pecan halves or plain pecan halves for garnish

serves 12–14

1 Preheat the oven to 350°F (180°C). Line the bottom of a 9-inch (23-cm) springform pan with a round of parchment paper.

2 To make the crust, in a food processor, pulse the pecans until coarsely ground. Add the gingersnap crumbs and brown sugar and pulse until the mixture is finely ground. Add the melted butter and process until moist clumps form. Scrape the crumb mixture into the prepared pan and, using your fingers, press it evenly into the pan bottom and about 1 inch (2.5 cm) up the sides. Refrigerate until firm, about 20 minutes.

3 To make the filling, in a food processor, process the cream cheese until smooth. Add the brown sugar and process until incorporated. Add the eggs, 1 at a time, processing until each one is incorporated. Add the cream, cornstarch, vanilla, cinnamon, ginger, nutmeg, and salt and process until evenly mixed. Add the pumpkin purée and process until smooth and well combined. Scrape the batter into the crust-lined pan and jiggle to even out the top of the filling.

4 Place the springform pan on a rimmed baking sheet. Bake until the edges of the cake are set and the center 2 inches (5 cm) of the cake is still wobbly, about 55 minutes. Transfer to a wire rack to cool completely, about 3 hours. Cover and refrigerate until chilled, about 4 hours.

5 About 1 hour before serving, remove the cake from the refrigerator. Remove the pan sides and carefully transfer the cake to a platter. Arrange candied pecans decoratively around the top edge. Let stand at room temperature about 1 hour. Cut into wedges and serve.

RICH IN FLAVOR from ground walnuts, buckwheat flour, and spices, this is a humble, though delicious cake. Since it's lighter than most gingerbreads, it's great to serve in the summer, topped with peaches that are bathed in a quick caramel sauce.

gingerbread & sautéed peaches

FOR THE CAKE

1⅓ cups (5½ oz/170 g) walnut pieces

½ cup (4 oz/125 g) buckwheat flour

1 teaspoon baking powder

¾ cup (6 oz/185 g) unsalted butter, at room temperature

½ cup (3½ oz/105 g) firmly packed brown sugar

1 tablespoon dark molasses

1 teaspoon pure vanilla extract

4 large eggs, separated

2 teaspoons ground ginger

1 teaspoon ground cinnamon

¼ teaspoon ground allspice

¼ teaspoon ground cloves

¼ teaspoon kosher salt

¼ teaspoon cream of tartar

6 tablespoons (3 oz/90 g) granulated sugar

Confectioners' sugar for dusting

Sautéed Peaches (page 124)
Whipped Cream (page 124)

serves 8 servings

1 To make the cake, preheat the oven to 325°F (165°C). Butter a 9-inch (23-cm) springform pan. Line the bottom of the pan with a round of parchment paper and butter the parchment.

2 In a food processor, combine the walnuts, buckwheat flour, and baking powder and pulse until the walnuts are finely ground. In a stand mixer fitted with the paddle attachment, beat the butter on medium speed until light, about 2 minutes. Add the brown sugar and beat until light and fluffy, about 2 minutes. Beat in the molasses and vanilla just until incorporated. Add the egg yolks, 1 at a time, beating until incorporated and scraping down the sides of the bowl as needed. Mix in the ginger, cinnamon, allspice, and cloves. Transfer the butter-sugar mixture to another large bowl.

3 Thoroughly clean the stand mixer bowl and add the egg whites. Fit the mixer with the whisk attachment, then beat the egg whites on medium speed until frothy. Add the salt and cream of tartar, increase the speed to medium-high, and beat until the whites hold their shape. Slowly add the granulated sugar, 1 tablespoon at a time, beating until soft peaks form. Using a rubber spatula, stir the walnut mixture into the butter-sugar mixture until blended. Fold one-third of the beaten egg whites into the batter to lighten it. Then gently fold in the remaining whites just until incorporated. Spoon into the prepared pan.

4 Bake the cake until springy to the touch and a tester inserted into the center comes out clean, about 45 minutes. Transfer the cake to a wire rack. Using a small, sharp knife, cut around the cake's edges to loosen. Let cool completely in the pan. If the edges of the cake are higher than the center, gently press down with your hands until the top is even. Remove the pan sides, transfer the cake to a platter, and dust with confectioners' sugar.

5 Cut the cake into wedges and spoon the warm sautéed peaches and caramel sauce over the top. Dollop with whipped cream. Serve right away.

pies & tarts

Coconut-Lime
Cream Pie **68**

Caramel-Nut Tartlets **71**

Pumpkin
Gingersnap Pie **72**

Broccoli & Goat
Cheese Quiche **73**

Sweet Pepper–
Manchego Quiche **75**

Apple Crumble Pie **76**

Pies and tarts are a

perfect way to end summer meals and holiday celebrations, and when I switched to a gluten-free lifestyle, I was determined not to give them up. Cream- or curd-based pies were easy to adapt, as they typically call for a crumb-type crust that could be made with ground nuts, gluten-free cookie crumbs, or toasted coconut. Traditional fruit pies and quiches proved a more challenging task, but once I learned the ins and outs of working with gluten-free flours and starches, I came up with a handful of tender and delicious crusts that could be used for a variety of different recipes. Sorghum flour, almond meal, and oats, all naturally gluten free, are my go-to ingredients for crisp toppings and thickening fillings.

Satisfy a craving with an easy-as-pie treat

The pies and tarts on the following pages suit a wide range of different occasions. The quiches are perfect for breakfast or brunch—even a casual lunch. The pumpkin and apple pies could easily anchor a holiday table, and no one will ever guess they are missing anything. The elegant nut tartlets can be varied in myriad ways and, since they're best served at room temperature, they can be made ahead of time for a special dinner party. The coconut-lime cream pie is a crowd pleaser, and will appeal to children and adults alike. I am particularly proud of my Basic Pie & Tart Dough (page 125), which took a lot of experimentation to perfect, but I am thrilled with the results. Use it as an all-purpose piecrust in any of your favorite baking recipes.

TANGY AND SWEET, this impressive pie offers an explosion of contrasting textures and flavors. A crunchy, spiced crust encloses a luxurious tart lime curd, billows of whipped cream come next, and then a sprinkle of crispy toasted coconut tops it off. My husband loves lime desserts, and he requested this recipe be included here.

coconut—lime cream pie

FOR THE LIME CURD

6 tablespoons (3 oz/90 g) unsalted butter, cut into ½-inch (12-mm) pieces

1 cup (8 oz/250 g) sugar

¾ cup (6 fl oz/180 ml) fresh lime juice (from about 6 large limes)

1 tablespoon grated lime zest

3 large eggs plus 3 large yolks

Ginger-Coconut Crust, page 125

Whipped Cream, page 124

¼ cup (¾ oz/20 g) unsweetened shredded coconut, toasted (see note)

serves 8

1 To make the lime curd, set a fine-mesh sieve over a bowl. In a heavy-bottomed saucepan over medium-high heat, combine the butter, sugar, lime juice, and lime zest, and cook, stirring, until the sugar dissolves and the mixture just comes to a simmer. In another bowl, whisk together the eggs and egg yolks.

2 Slowly whisk the hot lime mixture into the eggs, whisking constantly. Pour the lime-egg mixture back into the same saucepan and cook over medium-low heat, stirring constantly, until the curd thickens (do not boil), about 4 minutes. Immediately pour the curd into the sieve, pushing it through with a rubber spatula.

Let cool slightly in the bowl. Cover with plastic wrap, pressing it directly onto the surface of the curd. Refrigerate until chilled, at least 4 hours and up to 2 days.

3 Follow the instructions to make, bake, and cool the crust.

4 Scrape the cold lime curd into the crust-lined pan. Cover and refrigerate up to 8 hours, if you like.

5 Spread the whipped cream over the lime curd and sprinkle the toasted coconut over the top. Cut into wedges and serve.

✳ The lime curd can be made a day or two ahead, and the pie can be assembled early in the day. To toast coconut, preheat the oven to 300°F (150°C). Spread the coconut on a small baking sheet. Bake until golden brown, about 8 minutes. Let cool completely.

A CRUNCHY, SPICED chocolate crust is topped with caramel and nuts. It's an elegant dessert that is even better the second day. We offered many recipes like this one when I was the food editor at *Bon Appétit* magazine, and I was determined to come up with a gluten-free version.

caramel-nut tartlets

Chocolate Tartlet Dough, page 125

7 tablespoons (3½ oz/100 g) unsalted butter

½ cup (3½ oz/105 g) firmly packed brown sugar

3 tablespoons honey

1 cup (4½ oz/140 g) slivered almonds, toasted

¾ cup (4 oz/125 g) hazelnuts, toasted

¾ cup (3 oz/85 g) coarsely chopped walnuts, toasted

1½ tablespoons heavy cream

makes 6 tartlets

1 Prepare the dough as directed, shaping it in the pans and refrigerating it.

2 Preheat the oven to 350°F (180°C). Bake the crusts until they start to look dry, 10–12 minutes. Transfer the tartlet pans to a wire rack. If the crusts are puffed in places and/or if the sides have slid down, using a small rubber spatula, gently press on the dough to re-form the shell. Let the crusts cool completely, then place on a baking sheet.

3 In a saucepan over low heat, cook the butter, brown sugar, and honey, stirring constantly until the sugar dissolves and the mixture is no longer grainy. Raise the heat to high and continue to stir until the mixture comes to a boil. Boil without stirring until large bubbles form, about 1 minute. Remove from the heat. Stir in the almonds, hazelnuts, walnuts, and cream. Immediately pour into the crusts, dividing the filling evenly.

4 Bake until the filling bubbles, 12–15 minutes. Transfer to a wire rack to cool for about 30 minutes, then carefully remove the pan sides and let the tartlets cool completely. Serve at room temperature.

❊ Vary the nuts to your taste, using 2½ cups (about 12 oz/340 g) total. I've made it with cashews, pistachios, pecans, and blanched whole almonds. This can also be baked as one large tart: Instead of 4-inch (10-cm) tartlet pans, fit the crust into an 11-inch (28-cm) tart pan with removable sides. Bake the crust for 10–15 minutes, then bake the tart for 15–20 minutes. Cut the tart into 10–12 thin wedges.

GINGERSNAPS AND NUTS, crushed together, make a tempting crust that embraces a creamy filling laced with molasses, ginger, cinnamon, and nutmeg. Look no further than this recipe for your Thanksgiving pumpkin pie. But it's way too good to make only once a year. The pie is complete on its own, but my stepson loves it with a dollop of whipped cream on top.

pumpkin gingersnap pie

FOR THE CRUST

5 oz (155 g) gluten-free gingersnaps

1¼ cups (5 oz/155 g) pecan pieces

2½ tablespoons firmly packed brown sugar

5 tablespoons (2½ oz/75 g) unsalted butter, melted and cooled slightly

FOR THE FILLING

1 can (15 oz/470 g) pumpkin purée

¾ cup (6 oz/185 g) firmly packed brown sugar

2 tablespoons dark molasses

1 teaspoon ground ginger

½ teaspoon ground cinnamon

½ teaspoon ground nutmeg

¼ teaspoon kosher salt

3 large eggs

1¼ cups (10 fl oz/310 ml) heavy cream

1½ teaspoons pure vanilla extract

serves 8–10

1 Preheat the oven to 350°F (180°C).

2 To make the crust, in a food processor, pulse the gingersnaps, pecans, and brown sugar until the mixture is finely ground. Add the melted butter and process until moist clumps form. Scrape the crumb mixture into a 10-inch (25-cm) deep-dish glass pie dish and, using your fingers, press it evenly into the pan bottom and sides. Refrigerate the crust while preparing the filling.

3 To make the filling, in a large bowl, whisk together the pumpkin purée, brown sugar, molasses, ginger, cinnamon, nutmeg, and salt. Add the eggs and whisk until smooth. Whisk in the cream and vanilla. Scrape the filling into the crust-lined pan, smoothing the top.

4 Bake until the edges of the pie are puffy and the center is set, about 1 hour. Transfer to a wire rack to let cool completely. (This pie can be prepared 1 day ahead, then covered and refrigerated until serving.) Cut into wedges and serve at room temperature or chilled.

✻ Walnut halves or skinned hazelnuts can replace the pecans in this easy-to-make crust.

THE ALMOND MEAL crust of this quiche offers a slightly sweet and crunchy contrast to the savory custard filling. It was inspired by a recipe from Elana Amsterdam, who is an expert on cooking with almond flour. Made with ingredients that are available year-round, this is an excellent quiche recipe to have on hand for an impromptu Sunday brunch.

broccoli & goat cheese quiche

FOR THE CRUST
2 cups (9 oz/180 g) almond meal

¾ teaspoon baking soda

½ teaspoon kosher salt

⅓ cup (3 fl oz/80 ml) olive oil

FOR THE FILLING
3 cups (6 oz/185 g) broccoli florets

4 large eggs

1 cup (8 fl oz/250 ml) half-and-half

4 green onions, white and pale green parts, chopped

¼ teaspoon kosher salt

Generous ⅛ teaspoon rounded ground nutmeg

Freshly ground pepper

¾ cup (4 oz/125 g) fresh goat cheese, crumbled

serves 4–6

1 Place racks in the center and lower third of the oven and preheat to 350°F (180°C).

2 To make the crust, in a bowl, use a fork to stir together the almond meal, baking soda, and salt until blended. Add the oil and 1½ tablespoons water and stir together with the fork until evenly moist. Scrape the mixture into a 9-inch (23-cm) metal pie pan and, using your fingers, press it evenly into the pan bottom and sides.

3 Bake the crust until the edges begin to brown, 12–15 minutes. Set aside while preparing the filling.

4 To make the filling, cut the broccoli into 1-inch (2.5 cm) florets, then steam it over boiling water until crisp-tender, about 4 minutes. Transfer to a large bowl and cover with cold water to stop the cooking. Drain well.

5 Place the crust-lined pan on a rimmed baking sheet. In a glass measuring cup or bowl, beat the eggs with a fork until blended. Add the half-and-half, green onions, salt, nutmeg, and a generous amount of pepper and beat with a fork until blended. Place the broccoli florets in the crust and sprinkle the cheese over the top. Pour in enough of the egg mixture to fill the crust almost to the top.

6 Bake the quiche on the baking sheet until the custard is puffy, set, and trembles slightly in the center when you shake the pan, about 35 minutes. Let cool for about 20 minutes. Cut into wedges and serve warm.

✱ Cheddar or Gruyère cheese make good alternatives to the goat cheese. The quiche can also be made with the Basic Pie & Tart Dough (page 125).

FLAVORFUL AND CRISP, the mixed flour crust for this savory quiche is a versatile staple. To add a slightly nutty nuance, replace ¼ cup (¾ oz/25 g) of the sorghum flour with buckwheat flour. Manchego cheese, made from sheep's milk, is creamy and slightly piquant, but not too strong. Sharp Cheddar cheese would be a good alternative. I like to serve this for lunch, accompanied by a baby lettuce salad.

sweet pepper–manchego quiche

Basic Pie & Tart Dough, page 125

2 tablespoons olive oil

1 large red bell pepper, seeded and cut into ½-inch (12-mm) pieces

½ large yellow onion, cut into ½-inch (12-mm) pieces

Kosher salt and freshly ground pepper

4 large eggs

1 cup (8 fl oz/250 ml) half-and-half

2 teaspoons minced fresh thyme

1½ cups (4 oz/125 g) coarsely grated Manchego cheese or sharp Cheddar cheese

serves 4–6

1 Follow the instructions to make the dough, shaping it in the pan and trimming and crimping the edges. Preheat the oven to 375°F (190°C).

2 In a large nonstick frying pan over medium-high heat, warm the oil. Add the bell pepper and onion, season with salt and pepper, and sauté until coated with oil and warm, about 2 minutes. Cover the pan, reduce the heat to low, and cook, stirring occasionally, until the bell pepper and onion are tender, about 8 minutes. Uncover and remove from the heat.

3 Place the crust-lined pan on a rimmed baking sheet. In a glass measuring cup or bowl, beat the eggs with a fork until blended.

Add the half-and-half, thyme, ¼ teaspoon salt, and a generous amount of pepper and beat with a fork until blended. Place the bell pepper mixture in the crust and sprinkle the cheese over the top. Pour in enough of the egg mixture to fill the crust almost to the top.

4 Bake the quiche on the baking sheet until the eggs are puffy, set, and tremble slightly in the center when you shake the pan, 25–30 minutes. Let cool for about 20 minutes. Cut into wedges and serve warm.

✳ This quiche can be reheated in a 350°F (180°C) oven for about 20 minutes. The Almond Meal Crust in the broccoli quiche recipe would also be delicious with this filling. It will take a few more minutes to bake.

A CRISP, SWEET STRUESEL topping, a filling imbued with warm spices, and a tender crust: this is the ultimate apple pie. Look for special occasions to serve this beauty. The crust offers the gluten-free cook a real advantage; without gluten it won't become tough so it can't be overworked.

apple crumble pie

Basic Pie & Tart Dough, page 125

FOR THE FILLING

3 lb (1.5 kg) Granny Smith or pippin apples, peeled, halved, cored, and cut into scant ¼-inch (6-mm) slices

½ cup (4 oz/125 g) granulated sugar

2 tablespoons unsalted butter, melted

1 tablespoon cornstarch

2 teaspoons ground cinnamon

½ teaspoon ground allspice

Large pinch of kosher salt

FOR THE TOPPING

½ cup (1¾ oz/55 g) sorghum flour

½ cup (1½ oz/45 g) almond meal or sorghum flour

6 tablespoons (2¾ oz/85 g) firmly packed brown sugar

6 tablespoons (3 oz/90 g) granulated sugar

¼ teaspoon kosher salt

6 tablespoons (3 oz/90 g) cold unsalted butter, cut into ½-inch (12-mm) pieces

serves 8

1 Prepare the pie dough as directed, shaping it in the pan and refrigerating while you make the filling and topping. Place racks in the center and lower third of the oven and preheat to 400°F (200°C).

2 To make the filling, in a large bowl, combine the apples, granulated sugar, melted butter, cornstarch, cinnamon, allspice, and salt. Using a rubber spatula, toss to blend well. Let stand while you prepare the stirring, tossing occasionally.

3 To make the topping, in a food processor, process the sorghum flour, almond meal, brown sugar, granulated sugar, and salt until well combined. Add the butter and pulse until the mixture resembles wet sand.

4 Stir the filling and spoon it onto the crust, mounding the apples high in the center (they will be very high) and spooning any juices in the bowl over the top. Scatter the topping over the apples, covering them completely and pressing the topping gently to keep it in place.

5 Place the pie on the center rack and a rimmed baking sheet (I use a pizza pan) on the lower rack directly under the pie. Bake the pie for 35 minutes, covering the top of the pie loosely with aluminum foil if the topping is browning too quickly. Reduce the oven to 350°F (180°C) and continue baking until the apples are tender when pierced with a small sharp knife (do not cut through the bottom crust), 35–40 minutes longer. Transfer the pie to a wire rack and let cool at least 1½ hours. Serve warm or at room temperature.

✻ Thin apple slices become tender and juicy when baked. For easy cutting, slice them in food processor fitted with the thick slicing blade. It will take only a minute or two. If the crust softens while rolling, return it to the fridge for a few minutes to make it easier to work with.

puddings & custards

Pear Clafoutis.....................83

Salted Caramel
Pots de Crème 84

Indian Pudding....................86

Maple-Orange
Rice Pudding 87

Chai-Spiced Flan 88

Vanilla-Ginger
Crème Brûlée......................91

Creamy puddings, silky custards, rich pots de creme, and similar desserts are beloved comfort foods. When I switched to a gluten-free lifestyle, I rediscovered many of these naturally gluten-free desserts that I adored as a child and young adult. Now these indulgent treats are staples in my dessert repertory. Many of the recipes on these pages did not require modifying to make them gluten free, but I did re-examine the flavors so that they would be compatible with modern tastes. For example, the pots de crème have a deep caramel flavor and are topped with flaky sea salt; the flan is imbued with exotic chai-style spices; and the rice pudding features fragrant orange zest and chewy dried fruits.

End your meal with a luxurious treat

If your idea of dessert is rich, creamy, and comforting, look no further than the desserts in this chapter. Many are based on eggs, cream, or milk, which, when blended and baked, create soothing finales to any meal. (If you are sensitive to dairy products, a few of the recipes work well with nondairy milk). Other desserts include starchy, gluten-free grains like rice or cornmeal to add pleasing textures. For the clafoutis, which typically uses a touch of wheat flour for its structure, I used sorghum flour in its place. I like that sorghum flour is a whole-grain product, and its rustic taste added a new dimension to this classic dessert. Like many of my recipes, several can be made ahead of time, making them ideal for entertaining.

I FIRST TASTED clafoutis when I was interning at a restaurant in southern Vermont. It was like an alluring cross between a pancake and a pudding, punctuated with silky sweet pears, just like this version. I cut so many thin slices of the dessert for myself, I must have eaten half of it by the end of the evening. Anjou, red Anjou, and Bartlett pears all work well. The juice of a blood orange will give this an appealing rosy hue.

pear clafoutis

1½ lb (750 g) firm, ripe pears, peeled, cored, and cut ½-inch (12-mm) slices

⅔ cup (5 oz/155 g) sugar

2 tablespoons fresh orange juice

¾ cup (6 fl oz/180 ml) whole milk

6 tablespoons (3 fl oz/90 ml) heavy cream

6 tablespoons (1¼ oz/40 g) sorghum flour

4 large eggs

1 tablespoon pure vanilla extract

1 teaspoon grated lemon zest

⅛ teaspoon kosher salt

Confectioners' sugar for dusting

serves 6–8

1 Preheat the oven to 350°F (150°C). Butter a 10-inch (25-cm) deep-dish glass pie dish or similar sized baking dish.

2 Place the pear slices in a shallow baking dish, add ⅓ cup (2½ oz/80 g) of the sugar and the orange juice, and toss to combine. Let stand until the juices release, tossing occasionally, about 20 minutes. Pour out the juices into a small bowl, and reserve the pears and juices separately.

3 In a food processor, process the milk, cream, sorghum flour, eggs, vanilla, lemon zest, salt, the pear juices, and the remaining ⅓ cup sugar until very smooth, about 20 seconds. Pour enough of the batter into the pie dish to coat the bottom. Place in the oven and bake until just set, about 8 minutes.

4 Remove the pie dish from the oven and arrange the pear slices in a starburst pattern in the bottom of the pie dish. If there are any remaining pear juices in the bowl that held the pears, add it to the batter. Gently pour the remaining batter into the pie dish.

5 Bake until the custard puffs, the edges brown, and a small knife inserted into the center comes out clean, about 55 minutes. Let cool on a wire rack for at least 20 minutes and up to 2 hours.

6 Dust the clafoutis with confectioners' sugar. Cut into wedges and serve warm. Or, cover and refrigerate for up to 1 day and serve cold or at room temperature.

✳ To vary the flavor, the pears can be replaced with 3 cups (1½ lb/750 g) pitted cherries, 3 cups (12 oz/375 g) blueberries, or 3 cups (12 oz/375 g) blackberries.

RICH AND SILKY, with deep caramel flavor, these pots de crème are perfect for a special dinner. I bake these desserts in elegant pot de crème cups, so they need no garnish. If you want something on top, try a few fresh raspberries or chopped candied pecans.

salted caramel pots de crème

¾ cup (6 oz/185 g) sugar

1½ cups (12 fl oz/375 ml) heavy cream

½ cup (4 fl oz/125 ml) whole milk

6 large egg yolks

¼ teaspoon pure vanilla extract

⅛ teaspoon kosher salt

Fleur de sel or other flaky sea salt for sprinkling

serves 6

1 Preheat the oven to 325°F (165°C). Place six ⅔-cup (5–fl oz/160–ml) or ¾-cup (6-fl oz/180-ml) pots de crème cups, custard cups, or ramekins in a large roasting pan. Set a fine-mesh sieve over a large glass measuring cup. Bring a kettle of water to a boil.

2 In a large heavy-bottomed saucepan over low heat, stir together the sugar and ¼ cup (2 fl oz/60 ml) water until the sugar dissolves. Raise the heat to medium-high and boil, without stirring, until the mixture turns a deep amber color, occasionally brushing down the sides of the pan with a wet pastry brush and swirling the mixture in the pan, about 6 minutes. Gradually whisk in the cream and milk (the mixture will bubble vigorously), reduce the heat to medium, and then stir with a wooden spoon until all the caramel bits dissolve. Remove from the heat.

3 In a large bowl, whisk the egg yolks until frothy. Slowly add the hot caramel mixture, whisking constantly. Stir in the vanilla and kosher salt. Immediately pour the mixture into the sieve, then divide the mixture among the cups. dd enough hot water to the pan to come halfway up the sides of the cups. Cover the pan with foil.

4 Bake the pots de crème until they're just set around the edges but still move in the center when gently shaken, about 35 minutes. Carefully remove the cups from the pan and let cool completely on a wire rack. Cover and refrigerate for at least 2 hours or up to 2 days.

5 Sprinkle a pinch of fleur de sel over each pot de crème and serve cold.

✳ It is safest to caramelize the sugar in a heavy-bottomed pan that has a light-colored interior so you can observe the color of the boiling sugar as it browns. The darker the caramel gets, the deeper the flavor will be, but be careful not to burn it.

NUTTY CORNMEAL is the base for this naturally gluten-free dessert, inspired by a pudding I was served at Durgin Park, the New England restaurant I dined at during my college years in Boston. Pour a little milk or soy milk over a bowlful of leftover pudding and heat in the microwave for a satisfying breakfast.

"indian pudding"

Butter for the baking dish

5¼ cups (42 fl oz/1.3 l) whole milk or soy milk

⅔ cup (7 oz/220 g) light molasses

1¼ teaspoons ground ginger

½ teaspoon kosher salt

⅔ cup (2¾ oz/80 g) gluten-free whole-grain cornmeal such as Bob's Red Mill

Vanilla ice cream for serving

serves 6–8

1 Preheat the oven to 300°F (150°C). Butter a 7-by-11-inch (18-by-28-cm) glass baking dish.

2 In a large heavy-bottomed saucepan over medium-high heat, combine the milk, molasses, ginger, and salt. Bring to a simmer, stirring frequently with a wooden spoon. Gradually sprinkle the cornmeal over the hot milk mixture, stirring constantly. Reduce the heat to medium-low and simmer, stirring almost constantly, until the cornmeal is cooked, the mixture is thick but still pourable, and large bubbles form at the surface, about 15 minutes.

3 Pour the mixture into the prepared pan. Bake until a dark brown layer forms on top and the center no longer moves when the pan is shaken, about 1 hour and 30 minutes. Let cool in the pan for 10 minutes. Spoon the hot pudding into bowls. Top each with a scoop of ice cream and serve right away.

✳ Top this very thick, ginger- and molasses-laced pudding with a big scoop of vanilla ice cream; the contrast of the warm pudding and creamy cold ice cream is unforgettably comforting.

AN OLD-FASHIONED, diner-style dessert, this baked pudding is made by baking tender rice in a fragrant maple and orange custard. Delicious plain, it is even better when served with fresh berries. It is perfect for ending a weeknight family dinner. This pudding is good warm, at room temperature, or cold.

maple-orange rice pudding

½ cup (3½ oz/105 g) brown or white jasmine or basmati rice or other long-grain rice

2¼ cups (18 fl oz/560 ml) whole milk or nondairy milk

6 tablespoons (3 fl oz/90 ml) maple syrup, preferably grade B

3 large eggs plus 1 large egg yolk

1 teaspoon pure vanilla extract

¾ teaspoon grated orange zest

⅛ teaspoon kosher salt

¾ cup (4–5 oz/125–155 g) dried cranberries, raisins, dried cherries, or chopped dates

¼ teaspoon ground nutmeg

serves 6

1 In a small saucepan over high heat, bring 1 cup (8 fl oz/ 250 ml) water to a boil. Stir in the rice and bring to a simmer. Reduce the heat to low, cover, and cook until the water is absorbed, about 30 minutes for brown rice and 20 minutes for white rice. Turn off the heat and let stand, covered, for 5 minutes. Fluff the rice with a fork.

2 Preheat the oven to 325°F (165°C). Butter an 8-inch (20-cm) square glass baking dish or other shallow 2-qt (2-l) baking dish.

3 In a large bowl, whisk together the milk, maple syrup, eggs and egg yolk, vanilla, orange zest, and salt. Stir in the cranberries and cooked rice. Scrape the mixture into the prepared baking dish and sprinkle nutmeg on top.

4 Bring a kettle of water to a boil. Place the baking dish into a large roasting pan and add enough hot water to come halfway up the sides of the roasting pan.

5 Bake the pudding until a knife inserted into the center comes out clean, about 1 hour. Carefully remove the baking dish from the roasting pan and let cool on a wire rack for at least 15 minutes and up to 2 hours. Spoon the pudding into bowls and serve warm or at room temperature. Or, cover with plastic wrap and store in the refrigerator for up to 2 days.

✳ The dried cranberries can be replaced with raisins, dried cherries, or chopped dates. You can make this recipe with leftover rice—use 1½ cups (7½ oz/235 g) cooked rice and skip the first step.

ADDING FRAGRANT CHAI spices to a delicate flan transforms it into an exotic treat. I use cardamom pods, cloves, ginger, cinnamon sticks, and fennel seeds.

chai-spiced flan

1½ cups (12 fl oz/375 ml) whole milk

½ cup (4 fl oz/125 ml) heavy cream

10 whole cardamom pods

6 whole cloves

4 quarter-size slices peeled fresh ginger

Three 2-inch (5-cm) cinnamon sticks

1 teaspoon fennel seeds

½ cup (4 oz/125 g) granulated sugar

2 large eggs plus 2 large egg yolks

½ cup (3½ oz/105 g) firmly packed brown sugar

Pinch of kosher salt

serves 6

1 In a heavy-bottomed saucepan over medium heat, bring the milk, cream, cardamom pods, cloves, ginger, cinnamon sticks, and fennel seeds to a simmer. Turn off the heat, cover the pan, and let steep for 20 minutes.

2 Meanwhile, preheat the oven to 350°F (180°C). Place six ⅔-cup (5-fl oz/160-ml) or ¾-cup (6-fl oz/180-ml) custard cups or ramekins in a large roasting pan. Set a fine-mesh sieve over a large glass measuring cup. Bring a kettle of water to a boil.

3 In another saucepan over low heat, stir together the granulated sugar and ¼ cup (2 fl oz/60 ml) water until the sugar dissolves. Raise the heat to medium-high and boil, without stirring, until the syrup turns deep amber color, occasionally swirling the mixture in the pan and brushing down the pan sides with a wet pastry brush, about 8 minutes. Immediately divide the syrup among the custard cups. Working quickly and using oven mitts, tilt the cups to coat the bottoms with syrup.

4 In a bowl, whisk together the eggs and egg yolks. Return the milk mixture to a simmer. Slowly add the hot milk mixture to the eggs, whisking constantly. Immediately pour the mixture into the sieve. Add the brown sugar and salt to the strained milk mixture and stir until the sugar dissolves.

5 Divide the custard among the cups and add enough hot water to the pan to come halfway up the sides of the cups.

6 Bake the custards until set but the centers jiggle when the cups are gently shaken, about 30 minutes. Using a metal spatula, transfer the ramekins to wire racks. Let the custards cool for about 1 hour. Cover and refrigerate for at least 3 hours or up to 2 days.

7 Run a small sharp knife around the edge of each cup to loosen the custard. Invert the custards onto a platter or plates, shaking gently to release, and serve cold.

 Don't add the brown sugar to the custard before adding the eggs; if added too early, it may curdle the milk.

SILKY AND CRUNCHY, crème brûlée was my requested birthday dessert when I was a teenager. This one is based on my mom's creamy, vanilla-spiked recipe, with the addition of chewy nuggets of crystallized ginger. I like to nearly burn the sugar for a wonderfully crunchy topping.

vanilla-ginger crème brûlée

2 cups (16 fl oz/500 ml) heavy cream

¼ cup (2 oz/60 g) granulated sugar

1 vanilla bean, split lengthwise, or 1½ teaspoons pure vanilla extract

4 egg yolks

2–4 tablespoons finely chopped crystallized ginger

¼ cup (2 oz/60 g) firmly packed brown sugar

serves 6

1 Preheat the oven to 300°F (150°C). Place six ¾-cup (6–fl oz/180-ml) custard cups or ramekins in a large roasting pan. Set a fine-mesh sieve over a large glass measuring cup. Bring a kettle of water to a boil.

2 In a small heavy-bottomed saucepan, combine the cream and granulated sugar. Using the tip of a knife, scrape the vanilla seeds into the cream. Add the vanilla bean pod to the cream mixture and bring to a simmer over medium heat. Turn off the heat, cover the pan, and let steep for 15 minutes.

3 In a medium bowl, whisk the egg yolks until well blended. Return the cream mixture to a simmer over medium heat. Slowly add the hot cream mixture to the yolks, whisking constantly. (If using vanilla extract, stir into the custard.) Immediately pour the mixture into the sieve.

4 Scatter 1–2 teaspoons of ginger in each cup. Divide the custard among the cups and add enough hot water to the pan to come halfway up the sides of the cups.

5 Bake the crème brûlées until set but the centers jiggle when the cups are gently shaken, about 25 minutes. Using a metal spatula, transfer the ramekins to wire racks. Let the crème brûlées cool for about 30 minutes. Cover and refrigerate for at least 3 hours or up to 2 days.

6 Press the brown sugar through a fine-mesh strainer onto the crème brûlées, covering the surfaces completely. Using a kitchen torch, hold the flame 2 inches (5 cm) above the surface and heat until the sugar melts, bubbles, and browns, about 2 minutes. Alternatively, preheat the broiler. Place the ramekins on a rimmed baking sheet and place about 2 inches (5 cm) from the heat source. Heat until the sugar melts, bubbles, and browns, watching carefully, 2–4 minutes. Refrigerate the crème brûlées, uncovered, until the filling is cold and the topping is still brittle, at least 1 hour and up to 4 hours. Serve cold.

other desserts

Apple-Cranberry
Crumble.............................. **97**

Berry-Peach-
Cornmeal Crisp.................... **98**

Maple-Apple Trifles........... **100**

Maple-Berry Pavlova.......... **101**

Lemon-Berry
Meringue Nests................. **103**

Meringue Ice Cream
Sandwiches....................... **104**

Fresh fruit has always been a favorite choice for dessert. Many of the recipes in this chapter show how I incorporate seasonal fruits into my gluten-free lifestyle. For example, crisps make regular appearances in my kitchen. I comb the local farmers' market to find the freshest fruits for them, top the crisps with a mixture of oats, quinoa flakes, cornmeal, or nuts, along with butter and fragrant spices; then bake them until warm and crunchy. Meringues, too, are a great way to show off seasonal fruits, and I often form them into large pavlovas or individual nests, then I layer on whipped cream or citrus curd and fresh berries or other fruits for a light but elegant dessert. Meringues are also the perfect gluten-free base for decadent ice cream sandwiches.

Look to the seasons for dessert inspiration

This group of desserts defies categorization, but the common thread is that they are all naturally gluten free. Many of them are great ways to show off fresh, seasonal fruit, from berries to stone fruits, to pears, apples, and more. The desserts here are easy to vary, and I offer dozens of suggestions to customize them to the season or to your own taste. A well-stocked gluten-free pantry (see page 122) will come in handy when making the desserts in this chapter, as the recipes often call for oats, cornmeal, nuts, coconut, maple syrup, spices, and other items that store well. If you want to make the meringue nests, pavlova, or meringue ice cream sandwiches, be sure to read the troubleshooting tips on page 12 before you start.

SPICED WALNUT and brown sugar topping gilds this tempting dessert, which is perfect for a large gathering. As simple as it is delicious, if you bake this sweet-tart crumble right before a party, your friends will be greeted by its enticing aroma. Quinoa flakes create a lighter, less chewy crumble topping than traditional oats, but either works well. I love to eat leftovers for breakfast the next morning, with plain kefir poured over the top.

apple-cranberry crumble

FOR THE TOPPING

1¼ cups (4 oz/125 g) quinoa flakes or gluten-free rolled oats

1 cup (7 oz/220 g) plus 2 tablespoons firmly packed brown sugar

¾ cup (2¾ oz/80 g) sorghum flour

½ teaspoon ground cinnamon

½ teaspoon ground cardamom

¼ teaspoon kosher salt

¾ cup (6 oz/185 g) unsalted butter, at room temperature

¾ cup (3 oz/90 g) chopped walnuts

FOR THE FILLING

4 lb (2 kg) tart apples such as pippin or Granny Smith, peeled, quartered, cored, and sliced

3 cups (12 oz/375 g) fresh or frozen cranberries

⅔ cup (5 oz/155 g) granulated sugar

2 tablespoons tapioca flour

¾ teaspoon ground cinnamon

¾ teaspoon ground cardamom

Vanilla ice cream for serving

serves 8–10

1 Preheat the oven to 375°F (190°C). Butter a 13-by-9-by-2-inch (33-by-23-by-5-cm) glass or ceramic baking dish.

2 To make the topping, in a bowl, stir together the quinoa flakes, brown sugar, sorghum flour, cinnamon, cardamom, and salt. Add the butter and, using your fingers, rub the ingredients together until the mixture is the consistency of coarse crumbs. Stir in the walnuts.

3 To make the filling, in a large bowl, combine the apples, cranberries, granulated sugar, tapioca flour, cinnamon, and cardamom. Toss to mix well.

4 Pour the filling into the prepared baking dish (it will be very full) and spoon the topping evenly over the filling.

5 Bake until the topping is golden brown and the apples are tender when pierced with a small, sharp knife about 55 minutes, covering the crumble loosely with aluminum foil if the topping browns too quickly. Let cool for 20 minutes. Serve warm or at room temperature with scoops of ice cream.

✱ The sugary, crunchy topping offers a delightful contrast to the tart apple filling. If you prefer a sweeter filling, try Golden Delicious, Gala, or Fuji apples, instead of the pippin or Granny Smith I suggest here. Cardamom adds an exotic flavor, but ground ginger can be used in its place, or double the amount of cinnamon. If using frozen cranberries, there is no need to thaw them before using.

CRUNCHY CORNMEAL in the topping of this easy crisp adds pleasant texture and great flavor. I created this recipe to show off the fruit from the heirloom peach tree we harvest every summer. This crisp would be equally delicious with nectarines in place of the peaches and blueberries or raspberries instead of blackberries. Whatever the fruit, we like to serve this with vanilla ice cream.

berry-peach-cornmeal crisp

FOR THE TOPPING

¾ cup (2¾ oz/80 g) sorghum flour

⅔ cup (2¾ oz/80 g) gluten-free whole-grain cornmeal such as Bob's Red Mill

½ cup (2 oz/60 g) pecan pieces, toasted

½ cup (3½ oz/105 g) firmly packed brown sugar

¾ teaspoon ground cinnamon

¼ teaspoon ground ginger

½ cup (4 oz/125 g) cold unsalted butter, cut into ½-inch (12-mm) pieces

FOR THE FILLING

4 cups (1½ lb/750 g) sliced peeled peaches (from about 3 peaches)

3 cups (12 oz/375 g) fresh blackberries

⅓ cup (2½ oz/75 g) firmly packed brown sugar

2 tablespoons fresh lemon juice

1 tablespoon cornstarch

1 teaspoon pure vanilla extract

Vanilla ice cream for serving

serves 8

1 Place racks in the center and lower third of the oven and preheat to 375°F (190°C).

2 To make the topping, in a food processor, pulse the sorghum flour, cornmeal, pecans, brown sugar, cinnamon, and ginger until blended. Add the butter and pulse until the mixture starts to form clumps.

3 To make the filling, in a large bowl, combine the peaches, blackberries, brown sugar, lemon juice, cornstarch, and vanilla. Toss to mix well.

4 Pour the filling into an 11-by-7-inch (28-by-18-cm) baking dish or a shallow 2-quart (2-l) baking dish. Spoon the topping evenly over the filling.

5 Place the crisp on the center rack and a large baking sheet on the lower rack to catch any drips. Bake until the topping is golden brown and the peaches feel tender when pierced with a small, sharp knife, 35–40 minutes. Cool at least 20 minutes. Serve warm or at room temperature with scoops of ice cream.

 If you don't enjoy the extra crunch from the cornmeal, replace it with quinoa flakes or gluten-free oats.

HOMEMADE APPLESAUCE forms the base of *aeblekage*, a Danish dessert that layers bread crumbs with fruit sauce and tops it all with whipped cream. I've dressed up this treat by baking oats and almonds with maple syrup, and serving it in parfait glasses.

maple-apple trifles

1¾ cups (5½ oz/170 g) gluten-free rolled oats

¾ cup (4 oz/125 g) whole unblanched almonds, coarsely chopped

⅓ cup (3½ oz/105 g) maple syrup, preferably grade B

⅓ cup (2½ oz/75 g) firmly packed brown sugar

5 tablespoons (2½ oz/75 g) unsalted butter

¾ cup (6 fl oz/180 ml) cold heavy cream

1½ tablespoons granulated sugar

½ teaspoon pure vanilla extract

Applesauce, page 124

serves 6

1 Preheat the oven to 300°F (150°C). Butter a small rimmed baking sheet.

2 In a large bowl, stir together the oats and almonds. In a small heavy-bottomed saucepan over medium heat, cook the maple syrup, brown sugar, and butter, stirring constantly until the butter and sugar melt and the mixture bubbles. Pour the hot syrup over the oat-almond mixture and stir to coat. Scrape the mixture onto the prepared baking sheet.

3 Bake the maple-oat mixture until fragrant and browned, about 30 minutes. Let cool on the baking sheet. Using a spatula, break into clusters and transfer to an airtight container. Store at room temperature for up to 4 days.

4 Using an electric mixer, beat the cream in a bowl until soft peaks form. Add the granulated sugar and the vanilla and beat just to combine.

5 To assemble the trifles, spoon ⅓ cup (3 oz/90 g) of the applesauce into each of six 10-fl oz (315-ml) parfait glasses or rocks glasses. Top with half of the maple-oat mixture, dividing it evenly, followed by another ⅓ cup applesauce. Divide the remaining maple-oat mixture between the cups. Dollop each trifle with some of the whipped cream and serve right away.

✳ Grade B maple syrup has a richer flavor than grade A syrup, and will add a more distinct maple taste. Hazelnuts are just as good as almonds in this recipe. If there is any left the next morning, replace the whipped cream with plain kefir or yogurt for and a handful of fresh berries for a memorable breakfast.

WITH A CRISP SHELL and a marshmallow-like interior, this large, billowy meringue is topped with whipped cream mixed with a little Greek yogurt and then crowned with sweetened berries. In midsummer, swap the berries with peaches or nectarines.

maple-berry pavlova

1 cup (8 oz/250 g) plus
2 teaspoons sugar

2 teaspoons cornstarch

4 large egg whites, at room temperature

¼ teaspoon cream of tartar

1 teaspoon pure vanilla extract

¼ teaspoon kosher salt

Maple Yogurt Cream, page 124

Maple-Berry Topping, page 124

serves 6–8

1 Preheat the oven to 275°F (135°C). Line a baking sheet with parchment paper. Using an 8-inch (20-cm) round cake pan as a guide, draw an 8-inch (20-cm) circle on the parchment. Turn the parchment over on the sheet.

2 In a small bowl, stir together the 2 teaspoons sugar and the cornstarch. In a stand mixer, beat the egg whites on medium speed until frothy. Add the cream of tartar and beat on medium-high speed until soft peaks form, about 2 minutes. Gradually add the remaining 1 cup of sugar, 1 tablespoon at a time, beating constantly for about 3 minutes. Sprinkle with the cornstarch mixture and add the vanilla and salt and continue beating until very stiff, glossy, and the meringue holds a peak when the beater is lifted straight up, 1–2 minutes longer.

3 Dab a bit of the meringue underneath the corners of the parchment to secure it to the baking sheet. Using a rubber spatula, immediately mound the meringue in the center of the circle on the parchment. Spread the meringue to fill the circle, forming a shell with 2½-inch (6-cm) high sides and a wide well in the center.

4 Place the meringue in the oven, immediately reduce the oven temperature to 250°F (120°C), and bake for 45 minutes. Rotate the baking sheet, reduce the oven temperature to 200°F (95°C) and bake the meringue until dry, crisp, and firm on the outside but still soft inside, about 45 minutes longer. Turn off the oven and let cool in the oven for 1 hour. Let the meringue cool completely on the baking sheet on a wire rack. Peel off the parchment.

5 Gently transfer the meringue to a large platter. Spoon the Maple-Yogurt Cream in the center and top with Maple-Berry Topping. Cut into wedges and serve right away.

✱ The meringue can be baked 1 day ahead and stored in a turned-off oven. Or wrap the cooled meringue tightly and store at room temperature for up to 3 days. Do not make this dessert on a humid day.

ETHERIAL AND CRUNCHY, I came to love this, and other meringue-based desserts, when I started following a gluten-free diet. This dish features cardamom-scented crispy shells filled with a sumptuous, tart lemon curd made from Meyer lemons. Use any combination of berries, and other fresh fruits work well too.

lemon-berry meringue nests

1¼ cups (10 oz/300 g) plus 2 teaspoons sugar

¼ teaspoon ground cardamom (optional)

4 large egg whites, at room temperature

¼ teaspoon cream of tartar

1 teaspoon pure vanilla extract

Pinch of kosher salt

2 cups (8 oz/250 g) fresh strawberries, stemmed and quartered lengthwise

2 cups (8 oz/250 g) fresh blueberries

Yogurt–Meyer Lemon Curd, page 125

serves 8

1 Place racks in the upper and lower thirds of the oven and preheat to 200°F (95°C). Line 2 large baking sheets with parchment paper.

2 In a small bowl, stir together the 2 teaspoons sugar and the cardamom, if using. In a stand mixer, beat the egg whites on medium speed until frothy. Add the cream of tartar and beat on medium-high speed until soft peaks form, about 2 minutes. Gradually add 1 cup (8 oz/250 g) of the sugar, 1 tablespoon at a time, beating constantly. Sprinkle on the cardamom mixture and add the vanilla and salt and continue beating until stiff and glossy and the egg whites hold a peak when the beater is lifted straight up, 1–2 minutes longer.

3 Dab a bit of the meringue underneath the corners of the parchment papers to secure them to the baking sheets. Immediately spoon the meringue in eight mounds about ½ cup (4 fl oz/125 ml) each onto the prepared baking sheets. Using the back of a metal spoon, gently create a ¾ inch (2 cm) deep, wide well in the center of each mound.

4 Bake the meringues until dry, crisp, and firm, about 2 hours, switching the baking sheets halfway though. Turn off the oven and let the meringues cool completely in the closed oven, about 2 hours.

5 In a bowl, stir together the strawberries, blueberries, and the remaining ¼ cup (2 oz/60 g) sugar. Let stand at room temperature until juices form, about 30 minutes.

6 To serve, spoon about 3 tablespoons of the lemon curd into each meringue nest and top with the berries, dividing evenly. Serve right away.

LARGE SCOOPS of homemade ice cream served with sweet coconut meringues is a combination I remember from childhood and still adore. The coconut-flecked cookies here are crisp but delicate and pair well with the rich chocolate ice cream filling.

meringue ice cream sandwiches

2 large egg whites, at room temperature

⅛ teaspoon cream of tartar

½ cup (4 oz/125 g) sugar

1 teaspoon pure vanilla extract

Pinch of kosher salt

¾ cup (3 oz/90 g) unsweetened shredded coconut, toasted

1 pint (14 oz/440 g) chocolate ice cream, slightly softened (let stand at room temperature for 15 minutes)

serves 4

1 Preheat the oven to 225°F (110°C). Line a large baking sheet with parchment paper. Using a glass with a 3-inch (7.5-cm) wide rim as a guide, draw nine circles on the parchment. (There will be 1 extra meringue for the cook!). Turn the parchment over on the baking sheet.

2 In a stand mixer, beat the egg whites on medium speed until frothy. Add the cream of tartar and beat on medium-high speed until soft peaks form, about 2 minutes. Gradually add the sugar, 1 tablespoon at a time, beating constantly, for 1–2 minutes. Add the vanilla and salt and continue beating until stiff and glossy and the meringue holds a peak when the beater is lifted, 1–2 minutes longer. Fold in the toasted coconut.

3 Dab a bit of the meringue underneath the corners of the parchment to secure it to the sheet. Immediately spoon equal amounts of the meringue in the center of

each circle. Spread the meringue to fill the circles.

4 Bake the meringues until dry and crisp, about 1 hour and 15 minutes. Turn off the oven and let stand in the closed oven for 30 minutes. Cool the meringues completely on the baking sheet on a wire rack. Peel off the parchment. Store in an airtight container at room temperature for up to 2 days.

5 Transfer the meringues to a plate and freeze for 15 minutes. To assemble, arrange 1 meringue, smooth side up, on a work surface. Spoon a ½ cup (3½ oz/105 g) ice cream onto the meringue and spread to the edges. Top with the second meringue, smooth side down, and press gently. Using a spoon, smooth the ice cream around the edges. Cover with plastic wrap and return to the freezer. Repeat to make 4 sandwiches total. Freeze for at least 1 hour and up to 5 days. Serve frozen.

✳ You can vary the nuts in the meringue and the ice cream to suit your taste. Try walnut meringues with chocolate chip ice cream or pecan meringues with butterscotch ice cream.

breads

Seeded Irish Soda Bread....**110**

Whole Grain–Walnut
Bread **113**

Basic Corn Bread.................**114**

Chile-Cheese Corn Bread...**115**

Olive & Sage Flatbread.......**117**

Pumpkin-Date-Walnut
Bread...................................**118**

Chocolate Banana Bread...**120**

Crusty Millet Loaf..............**121**

When I changed my eating habits for good, I was determined to find a way to continue to enjoy artisan-style, crusty breads and other baked goods that typically rely on wheat flour for their structure and texture. Developing the recipes for this book offered me the opportunity to experiment with a wide range of gluten-free flours and starches, aiming for the perfect combination of ingredients to achieve the desired result. On the pages that follow, you'll find loaves for any occasion, from sweet quick breads, to savory soda breads and corn breads, to flat breads perfect for hors d'oeuvres, to all-purpose loaves to have on hand for any occasion.

Make your next loaf of bread a homemade one

Unless you live in an area that has a high demand for gluten-free products, it can be hard to find quality gluten-free breads in your local bakery or supermarket. And even if you do have access to delicious breads nearby, there's nothing like the smell and taste of freshly baked loaves from your own oven. The recipes on the following pages all feature customized blends of flours and starches that deliver the flavor and texture I look for in a great loaf of bread: you'll find crusty, seeded loaves for slicing and topping with savory spreads; a tender, olive- and herb-spiked flat bread perfect for dipping into olive oil; rustic corn breads for serving alongside soups or stews; and sweet quick breads that quell hunger as an afternoon snack or quick breakfast.

OATS AND SEEDS fill this hearty loaf, and you will not miss the wheat. It is great warm or at room temperature, spread with butter and preserves, or butter and smoked salmon. It also makes an ideal accompaniment to steaming bowls of chowder.

seeded irish soda bread

½ cup (1¾ oz/50 g) sorghum flour, plus more for dusting

¾ cup (6 fl oz/180 ml) plus 3 tablespoons whole milk, low-fat milk, or soy milk

1 tablespoon distilled white vinegar

1 large egg

1 cup (2¾ oz/80 g) gluten-free oat flour

½ cup (2½ oz/75 g) potato starch

2 tablespoons firmly packed brown sugar

2 teaspoons xanthan gum

1½ teaspoons baking powder

1 teaspoon baking soda

1 teaspoon kosher salt

¼ cup (2 oz/60 g) cold unsalted butter, cut into ½-inch (12-mm) pieces

3 tablespoons gluten-free oat bran

2 tablespoons flaxseed meal

⅓ cup (1½ oz/45 g) shelled sunflower seeds or pumpkin seeds

1½ teaspoons chia or poppy seeds (optional)

makes 1 loaf

1 Preheat the oven to 375°F (190°C). Grease an 8- to 9-inch (20- to 23-cm) round cake pan and dust with sorghum flour.

2 In a glass measuring cup, combine the milk and vinegar. Let stand until thickened, about 5 minutes. Add the egg and whisk with a fork until blended.

3 In a food processor, combine the oat flour, sorghum flour, potato starch, brown sugar, xanthan gum, baking powder, baking soda, and salt and process until blended. Add the butter and pulse until the mixture resembles fine meal. Add the oat bran and flaxseed meal and pulse just until blended.

4 Transfer the mixture to a bowl and stir in the sunflower seeds. Add the liquid ingredients and, using a rubber spatula, mix until a sticky batter forms.

5 Scrape the batter into the prepared pan. Dip the spatula into room temperature water and use it to form a smooth round loaf. Flatten slightly. Using a sharp knife, score a ¼-inch (6-mm) cross on top of the loaf that extends to the edges. Sprinkle the loaf with chia seeds.

6 Bake until the loaf is slightly browned, sounds hollow when tapped, and bamboo skewer inserted into the center comes out clean, about 50 minutes. Transfer to a wire rack and let cool in the pan for 5 minutes, then turn out onto the rack and let cool. Serve warm or at room temperature. Store wrapped airtight at room temperature for up to 2 days.

❋ Sunflower seeds can occasionally turn green when baked. The greenish tinge is harmless, and makes this bread a good candidate to serve on St. Patrick's Day. The seeds in my soda bread didn't turn green until a day or two after baking. To avoid this, replace the sunflower seeds with pumpkin seeds, any nut you like, or raisins. If you don't have both oat bran and flaxseed meal, it's OK to use 5 tablespoons total of whichever is in your cupboard.

THIS WHOLESOME LOAF is the bread I keep on hand for everyday eating. I like it for breakfast—toasted or untoasted. I also serve it alongside salads or soups, spread it with soft cheese, or smear it with avocado. A favorite preparation of mine is to top it with burrata cheese and sliced radishes. The buckwheat gives it an earthy flavor, but if you like, replace it with another ¼ cup (1 oz/30 g) quinoa flour.

whole grain–walnut bread

1 cup (3½ oz/105 g) sorghum flour, plus more for dusting

¾ cup (6 fl oz/180 ml) plus 3 tablespoons low-fat milk, whole milk, or soy milk

1 tablespoon distilled white vinegar

1 large egg

¼ cup (1 oz/30 g) buckwheat flour

¼ cup (1 oz/30 g) quinoa flour

¼ cup (1¾ oz/40 g) potato starch

¼ cup (1 oz/30 g) tapioca flour

2 tablespoons firmly packed dark or golden brown sugar

2 teaspoons xanthan gum

1½ teaspoons baking powder

1 teaspoon baking soda

1 teaspoon kosher salt

¼ cup (2 oz/60 g) cold unsalted butter, cut into ½-inch (12-mm) pieces

⅓ cup (1⅓ oz/40 g) flaxseed meal

⅓ cup (1½ oz/45 g) chopped walnuts

1½ teaspoons toasted sesame seeds or untoasted chia seeds (optional)

makes 1 loaf

1 Preheat the oven to 375°F (190°C). Grease an 8- to 9-inch (20- to 23-cm) round cake pan and dust with sorghum flour.

2 In a glass measuring cup, combine the milk and vinegar. Let stand until thickened, about 5 minutes. Add the egg and whisk with a fork until blended.

3 In the bowl of a food processor, combine the sorghum flour, buckwheat flour, quinoa flour, potato starch, tapioca flour, brown sugar, xanthan gum, baking powder, baking soda, and salt and process until blended. Add the butter and pulse until the mixture resembles a fine meal. Add the flaxseed meal and pulse once to mix in.

4 Transfer the mixture to a bowl and stir in the walnuts. Add the liquid ingredients and, using a rubber spatula, mix until a sticky batter forms. Scrape the batter into the prepared pan. Dip the spatula into room temperature water and use to form a smooth round loaf. Flatten slightly. Using a sharp knife, score a ¼-inch (6-mm) cross on top of the loaf that extends to the edges. Sprinkle the loaf with sesame seeds.

5 Bake until the loaf is slightly browned, sounds hollow when tapped, and a bamboo skewer inserted into the center comes out clean, about 50 minutes. Transfer to a wire rack and let cool in the pan for 5 minutes, then turn out onto the rack and let cool. Serve warm or at room temperature. Store wrapped airtight at room temperature for up to 3 days or refrigerate for up to 5 days.

✳ Try flavoring the bread with 2 teaspoons fennel seeds and/or replace the walnuts with pecans or hazelnuts.

SLIGHTLY SWEET, this satisfying corn bread has abundant corn flavor. Choose a whole-grain cornmeal such as Bob's Red Mill for the best taste. I serve this with chili or soup, or at brunch with eggs. Leftovers are great for a quick breakfast, or spread with peanut butter for a nourishing snack.

basic corn bread

¾ cup (6 fl oz/180 ml) plus 3 tablespoons low-fat milk, whole milk, or soy milk

1 tablespoon distilled white vinegar

6 tablespoons (3 fl oz/90 ml) olive oil

1 large egg

1 cup (3¾ oz/120g) gluten-free whole-grain cornmeal such as Bob's Red Mill

½ cup (1¾ oz/50 g) sorghum flour

¼ cup (1¼ oz/40 g) potato starch

¼ cup (1 oz/30 g) tapioca flour

⅓ cup (2½ oz/75 g) firmly packed brown sugar

2½ teaspoons baking powder

1 teaspoon kosher salt

¾ teaspoon xanthan gum

½ teaspoon baking soda

Freshly ground pepper

makes 8–12 servings

1 Preheat the oven to 375°F (190°C). Brush an 11-by-7-by-2-inch (28-by-18-by-5-cm) glass baking dish with olive oil.

2 In a glass measuring cup, combine the milk and vinegar. Let stand until thickened, about 5 minutes. Add the oil and egg and whisk with a fork until blended.

3 In a large bowl, whisk together the cornmeal, sorghum flour, potato starch, tapioca flour, brown sugar, baking powder, salt, xanthan gum, baking soda, and a generous amount of pepper. Add the liquid ingredients to the dry ingredients and mix well with a wooden spoon.

4 Pour the batter into the prepared pan, spreading evenly with a rubber spatula, and smoothing the top.

5 Bake the bread until brown, springy to the touch, and a toothpick inserted into the center comes out clean, about 30 minutes. Transfer the corn bread to a wire rack and let cool in the pan for 15 minutes. Serve warm or at room temperature.

❋ For an herbed corn bread, add dried rosemary, marjoram, or sage. For a festive brunch bread, I add ¾ cup (4½ oz/140 g) raisins or ¾ cup (4 oz/125 g) chopped dried figs, ¾ cup (3 oz/90 g) dried cranberries, and 2 tablespoons crushed fennel seeds. The blend of potato starch and tapioca flour gives this bread a lovely texture. If you don't have both starches in your pantry, use ½ cup (2–2½ oz/60–80 g) of either one. It's also the perfect base for corn bread stuffing: Just cut the bread into ¾-inch (2-cm) cubes, brown in a 350°F (180°C) oven, and mix with your favorite stuffing ingredients.

EASY TO MAKE, this bread relies mostly on whole-grain cornmeal and sorghum flour for its tender texture and full flavor. I like to serve it with stews, soups, or eggs. It is best warm, but keeps for at least 2 days. If made ahead, wrap squares of the bread in paper towels and reheat briefly in the microwave.

chile-cheese corn bread

6 tablespoons olive oil, plus oil for the baking dish

1 cup (6 oz/185 g) fresh corn kernels (cut from about 2 ears of corn)

3 serrano chiles, seeded and finely chopped

¾ cup (6 fl oz/180 ml) plus 3 tablespoons low-fat milk, whole milk, or soy milk

1 tablespoon distilled white vinegar

1 large egg

1¼ cups (4¾ oz/150 g) gluten-free whole-grain cornmeal, such as Bob's Red Mill

½ cup (1¾ oz/50 g) sorghum flour

⅓ cup (2½ oz/75 g) firmly packed brown sugar

¼ cup (1 oz/30 g) tapioca flour or ¼ cup (1¼ oz/40 g) potato starch

2½ teaspoons baking powder

1½ teaspoons dried marjoram

1 teaspoon kosher salt

¾ teaspoon xanthan gum

½ teaspoon baking soda

Freshly ground pepper

¼ lb (125 g) Manchego or extra-sharp Cheddar cheese, grated

makes 8–12 servings

1 Preheat the oven to 400°F (200°C). Brush an 11-by-7-by-2-inch (28-by-18-by-5-cm) glass baking dish with olive oil. In a frying pan over medium-high heat, warm 1 tablespoon of the olive oil. Add the corn and chiles and sauté until beginning to brown, about 4 minutes. Let cool.

2 In a glass measuring pitcher, combine the milk and vinegar. Let stand until thickened, about 5 minutes. Add the remaining 5 tablespoons of the olive oil and the egg and whisk with a fork until blended.

3 In a large bowl, whisk together the cornmeal, sorghum flour, brown sugar, tapioca flour, baking powder, marjoram, salt, xanthan gum, baking soda, and a generous amount of pepper. Add the liquid ingredients to the dry ingredients and stir until combined. Stir in the corn-chile mixture and the cheese.

4 Pour the batter into the prepared pan, spreading evenly with a rubber spatula, and smoothing the top. Bake the bread until brown, springy to the touch, and a toothpick inserted into the center comes out clean, about 25 minutes. Transfer the corn bread to a wire rack and let cool in the pan for 15 minutes. Serve warm or at room temperature.

✳ This is also good without the cheese. For a colorful variation, chop a red bell pepper and sauté it for 5 minutes before adding the corn and chiles to the frying pan. Leftovers make a quick satisfying breakfast or snack.

WHOLE-GRAIN CORNMEAL gives this bread a taste and texture similar to semolina bread. I use it to dip into my favorite extra-virgin olive oil, or I serve it alongside pasta with fresh clam sauce to soak up the briny juices. This bread is great toasted the next day, or sliced, brushed with olive oil, and grilled.

olive & sage flatbread

2 tablespoons extra-virgin olive oil, plus oil as needed

2 tablespoons minced fresh sage

1 cup (3¾ oz/110 g) brown rice flour

¾ cup (3 oz/90 g) gluten-free whole-grain cornmeal, such as Bob's Red Mill

½ cup (2½ oz/75 g) potato starch

¼ cup (1 oz/30 g) buckwheat flour

1 tablespoon firmly packed brown sugar

1½ teaspoons kosher salt

1½ teaspoons rapid-rise yeast

1¼ teaspoons xanthan gum

1 cup (8 fl oz/250 ml) very warm water (120°–130°F/49°–54°C)

2 large eggs, at room temperature

¼ cup (4 oz/125 g) pitted Kalamata olives, chopped

Freshly ground pepper

makes 1 loaf

1 In a small heavy-bottomed saucepan over medium heat, warm 2 tablespoons of the oil and 1½ tablespoons of the sage until fragrant, about 1 minute. Remove from the heat.

2 In a large bowl, whisk together the rice flour, cornmeal, potato starch, buckwheat flour, brown sugar, salt, yeast, and xanthan gum. Add the warm water and using a sturdy wooden spoon, stir until combined (the mixture will be very thick). Add in the eggs, one at a time, stirring until each one is incorporated. Stir in the oil-sage mixture until a thick, smooth batter forms. Stir in the olives.

3 Line a large baking sheet with parchment paper. Using a rubber spatula, spread the batter on the paper into an 8-by-12-inch (20-by-30-cm) oval. Brush generously with olive oil and sprinkle with plenty of pepper and the remaining ½ tablespoon sage. Let the dough rise in a warm spot until puffy, about 1 hour.

4 Preheat the oven to 400°F (200°C). Bake the bread until deep brown and firm to the touch, about 25 minutes. Transfer the bread to a wire rack and let cool for at least 15 minutes. Cut into slices and serve warm or at room temperature.

✳ Rosemary can replace the sage. Rice flour gives this bread structure, cornmeal offers rich flavor, and buckwheat provides earthiness. However, feel free to experiment with different flours, just keep the proportions the same. A mixture of sorghum and quinoa flours can replace the cornmeal. Try millet flour too. This recipe can also be made into 2 small loaves: Using a rubber spatula, spoon the dough onto a parchment-lined baking sheet in 2 mounds and shape into 6½-by-4½-inch (16.5-by-11.5-cm) ovals. Using a sharp knife, score each loaf crosswise 4 times. Bake until the loaves sound hollow when tapped, about 30 minutes.

PLUMP AND TENDER, this tea bread is equally welcome as breakfast or dessert. Flavored with pumpkin pie spices and a touch of dark molasses, it is not too sweet, yet is still cakelike. I love to spread fresh ricotta or burrata cheese over slices.

pumpkin-date-walnut bread

1¼ cups (3¾ oz/120 g) sorghum flour

1¼ cups (9 oz/280 g) firmly packed brown sugar

1 cup (5 oz/145 g) potato starch

¾ cup (2¼ oz/70 g) almond meal

1¼ teaspoons xanthan gum

1 teaspoon baking powder

1 teaspoon baking soda

1 teaspoon ground cinnamon

1 teaspoon ground ginger

½ teaspoon kosher salt

¼ teaspoon ground cloves

1¼ cups (11½ oz/295 g) canned pumpkin purée

½ cup (4 fl oz/125 ml) olive oil

3 large eggs

1 tablespoon dark (full-flavored) molasses (optional)

1 teaspoon pure vanilla extract

1 cup (4 oz/125 g) chopped walnuts

1 cup (6 oz/185 g) chopped pitted dates

makes 1 loaf

1 Preheat the oven to 350°F (180°C). Line a 9-inch (23-cm) metal loaf pan with parchment paper, allowing the paper to extend 2 inches (5 cm) beyond the long sides of the pan. Grease the short sides of the pan.

2 In a large bowl, whisk together the sorghum flour, brown sugar, potato starch, almond meal, xanthan gum, baking powder, baking soda, cinnamon, ginger, salt, and cloves. In another bowl, whisk together the pumpkin, oil, eggs, molasses (if using), and vanilla. Add the pumpkin mixture to the sorghum flour mixture. Using an electric mixer, beat until the batter is smooth and silky, about 2 minutes. Stir in the walnuts and dates. Transfer the batter to the prepared pan.

3 Bake until the loaf is firm to the touch and a bamboo skewer inserted into the center comes out clean, about 1 hour 25 minutes.

4 Transfer to a wire rack and let cool in the pan for 10 minutes. Using the parchment paper, lift the bread from the pan and transfer to the wire rack. Remove the parchment paper from the sides, leaving it under the bread. Let cool completely on the rack, then remove the parchment from the bottom. Wrap the bread tightly in foil and refrigerate for up to 5 days or freeze up to 1 month. Using a serrated knife, cut into slices and serve. Serve cold or at room temperature.

✱ The loaf is large, so be certain to test for doneness with a long tester that can reach all the way through. I use a bamboo skewer. This bread freezes well, so it can be made way ahead. The nuts and dried fruit can be varied to your taste. I also like toasted hazelnuts or pecans, and diced dried pears or raisins. This loaf can be transformed into gingerbread by upping the ginger to 2 teaspoons.

A DARK CHOCOLATE banana bread I once developed for *Bon Appétit* magazine inspired this loaf, and this is every bit as good. Cocoa powder is a gluten-free ingredient that adds both texture and flavor to baked goods. This is a perfect treat for Sunday brunch, and leftovers keep well in the fridge.

chocolate banana bread

1 cup (7 oz/220 g) firmly packed brown sugar

½ cup (1¾ oz/50 g) sorghum flour

½ cup (1¾ oz/50 g) tapioca flour

½ cup (2½ oz/70 g) potato starch

½ cup (1½ oz/45 g) unsweetened cocoa powder

1¼ teaspoons ground cinnamon

1 teaspoon xanthan gum

1 teaspoon baking powder

½ teaspoon baking soda

½ teaspoon kosher salt

3 large very ripe bananas, peeled and cut into pieces

About ½ cup (4 oz/125 g) plain yogurt

2 large eggs

1 teaspoon pure vanilla extract

½ cup (4 oz/125 g) unsalted butter, melted and cooled slightly

1 cup (6 oz/185 g) bittersweet or semisweet chocolate chips

makes 1 large loaf

1 Preheat the oven to 350°F (180°C). Line 9-inch (23-cm) glass loaf pan with parchment paper, allowing the paper to extend at least 2 inches (5 cm) beyond the long sides of the pan. Grease the short sides of the pan.

2 In a large bowl, whisk together the brown sugar, sorghum flour, tapioca flour, potato starch, cocoa powder, cinnamon, xanthan gum, baking powder, baking soda, and salt. In the bowl of a food processor, purée the bananas until smooth.

3 Transfer the purée to a glass measuring cup and add enough yogurt to measure 1¾ cups (14 fl oz/415 ml). Whisk in the eggs and vanilla. Add the yogurt mixture and the melted butter to the dry ingredients and stir with a rubber spatula until well combined. Fold in the chocolate chips.

4 Spoon the batter into the prepared pan. Bake the bread until firm to the touch and a small sharp knife inserted into the center comes out clean, about 1 hour and 5 minutes. Transfer the bread to a wire rack and let cool in the pan for 10 minutes. Using the parchment paper, lift the bread from the pan and transfer to the wire rack. Remove the parchment paper from the sides, leaving it under the bread. Let cool on the rack for 20 minutes, then remove the remaining parchment and let cool completely. Wrap the bread tightly in foil and refrigerate for up to 5 days or freeze up to 1 month. Using a serrated knife, cut into slices and serve cold or at room temperature.

✱ This makes a big loaf, and sometimes I freeze half to have on hand for impromptu visitors.

GREAT, CRUSTY BRE
so I developed this one, in
Brown and Jim Lahey. The
can be wrapped and refrig
Use for toast, or grill slices, bi
bruschetta. Sauté day-old cube   n   s.

crusty millet loaf

1 tablespoon chia seeds, ground in a spice mill

1 cup (8 fl oz/250 ml) warm water (110°–115°F/43°–46°C)

1 tablespoon sugar

1 package (2¼ teaspoons/ ¼ oz/7 g) active dry yeast

⅔ cup (3½ oz/105 g) millet flour, plus more as needed

½ cup (1¾ oz/50 g) sorghum flour

⅓ cup (1½ oz/45 g) cornstarch

⅓ cup (1¾ oz/50 g) potato starch

¼ cup (1¼ oz/35 g) tapioca flour

¾ teaspoon xanthan gum

¾ teaspoon kosher salt

1 tablespoon olive oil

Sesame seeds (toasted or untoasted) or chia seeds for sprinkling

makes 1 large loaf

1 Put the ground chia seeds in the bowl of a stand mixer fitted with the paddle attachment. Add ½ cup (4 fl oz/125 g) of the warm water, the sugar, and yeast and stir until well combined. Let stand until foamy, about 10 minutes.

2 In a bowl, whisk together the ⅔ cup millet flour, the sorghum flour, cornstarch, potato starch, tapioca flour, xanthan gum, and salt. Add the remaining ½ cup (4 fl oz/125 g) warm water and the oil to the yeast mixture. Gradually beat in the dry ingredients on low speed until well combined. Increase the speed to high and beat until the dough is the consistency of whipped cream, about 4 minutes. Mix in more millet flour, a tablespoon at a time, to thicken the dough if necessary.

3 Cut a piece of parchment paper to fit inside a 6- to 8-quart (5.5- to 7.5-l) heavy-bottomed pot with a tight-fitting lid. Place the parchment on a work surface. Using a rubber spatula, transfer the

dough to the parchment and shape into a 7-by-5-inch (18-by-13-cm) oval. Dip the spatula in water and smooth the top. Using a sharp knife, score the loaf crosswise 3 or 4 times. Sprinkle the loaf with sesame seeds. Lightly oil a large bowl and invert it so that it covers the loaf. Let the dough rise for 30 minutes.

4 Cover the pot and place in the oven. Heat the oven to 400°F (200°C). Let the dough continue to rise on the work surface until puffy, about 30 minutes longer.

5 Using oven mitts, remove the pot from the oven and remove the lid. Transfer the bread on the parchment to the pot. Cover the pot and return to the oven. Bake the loaf for 30 minutes. Uncover the pot and continue baking until the bread is brown and sounds hollow when tapped on the bottom, about 15 minutes longer. Turn out onto a wire rack, remove the parchment, and let cool at least 30 minutes. Serve warm or at room temperature.

 For an earthier flavor, replace 2–4 tablespoons of the sorghum flour with buckwheat flour.

a gluten-free pantry

I have found that having a good supply of pantry staples on hand provides a solid foundation for putting together tempting goodies whenever I feel like baking. Stocking the pantry requires a little extra thought when you are living a gluten-free lifestyle, but if your cupboard is filled with the items you use regularly, you will just need to shop for any fresh ingredients that you don't have.

The following checklist features the pantry items that I rely on for the recipes in this book. Use it to take inventory of what you have in stock, or as a template for customizing your own gluten-free baking pantry.

If you or a loved one has a gluten intolerance or sensitivity, you'll want to take extra care when buying pantry ingredients. Be sure to always read the package labels. Even some things that are naturally gluten-free are sometimes made in facilities that fashion products that contain gluten and can become contaminated during manufacturing or packaging. Also, products can change, so check labels frequently.

Gluten-free staples

To achieve the desired texture and flavor in gluten-free baked goods, it is common to use a combination of different flours and starches to achieve great results. See the list on pages 9–11 of versatile gluten-free flours and starches, whole grains, flakes, and meals, and other items to have on hand in your pantry.

NUTS AND SEEDS

□ almonds

□ hazelnuts

□ pecans

□ pistachios

□ walnuts

□ almond and peanut butter

□ chia seeds

□ sesame seeds

□ sunflower seeds

CHOCOLATE

□ bittersweet or semisweet

□ chocolate chips

□ unsweetened cocoa powder

SPICES AND EXTRACTS

□ coarse kosher salt

□ black peppercorns

□ allspice

□ cardamom

□ cinnamon

□ cloves

□ ginger

□ nutmeg

□ almond extract

□ vanilla extract

SWEETENERS

□ confectioners' sugar

□ dark molasses

□ golden or dark brown sugar

□ granulated sugar

□ honey

□ maple syrup, preferably grade b

OTHER INGREDIENTS

□ baking powder and baking soda

□ cream of tartar

□ crystallized ginger

□ distilled white vinegar

□ dried fruit

□ eggs

□ rice

□ shredded or flaked coconut

□ yeast

Organizing the pantry

Once you set up your gluten-free pantry, you'll have many bags of gluten-free ingredients. I have two suggestions for how to organize them:

- Put a clip on each bag and keep the bags in a basket with a handle. Grab the basket whenever you are baking.
- Transfer the flours to large canning jars or other storage containers and label clearly. Although this method is neater, I prefer keeping the ingredients in their bags so I can check the useful information on the labels.

Gluten-free sources

The following are some of my favorite products and stores for gluten-free baking. While availability varies, many stores now have gluten-free sections.

BOB'S RED MILL
For most flours, starches, whole grains, flakes and meals, and xanthan gum
www.bobsredmill.com/gluten-free

ARROWHEAD MILLS
Especially great for buckwheat and millet flours
www.arrowheadmills.com/category/gluten-free

ANCIENT HARVEST
For quinoa flakes
ancientharvest.com/

TRADER JOES
For gluten-free ginger snaps, almond meal, gluten-free oats, and nuts
www.traderjoes.com

WHOLE FOODS
For most of the above items
www.wholefoods.com

basic recipes

WILD BLUEBERRY SAUCE

1 package (1 lb/500 g) frozen wild blueberries (not thawed)

⅔ cup (7 oz/220 g) maple syrup, preferably grade B

1 tablespoon plus 1 teaspoon cornstarch

1 tablespoon plus 1 teaspoon water

¾ teaspoon grated lemon zest

¼ teaspoon grated nutmeg

In a heavy saucepan over medium heat, bring 2½ cups (11 oz/ 310 g) of the blueberries and the maple syrup to a simmer. Cook until the berries begin to soften, about 3 minutes. In a small bowl, dissolve the cornstarch in the water and stir into the sauce. Simmer, stirring constantly, until the sauce thickens slightly. Remove from the heat and immediately stir in the remaining berries (about 1¼ cups/5 oz/155 g), the lemon zest, and nutmeg. Let cool for 20 minutes. Cover and refrigerate until chilled, about 2 hours. Makes 3 cups (12 oz/375 g).

SAUTÉED PEACHES

1½ tablespoons unsalted butter

3 cups (18 oz/560 g) peeled and sliced fresh peaches (from 2 or 3 peaches)

¼ cup (2 oz/60 g) firmly packed brown sugar

In a large nonstick skillet over medium heat, melt the butter. Add the peaches and cook until warmed through, stirring frequently, about 2 minutes. Add the brown sugar and cook, stirring, until melted and the syrup thickens slightly, about 2 minutes. Serve warm. Makes 2 cups (16 fl oz/500 ml).

Note: Nectarines would also work well here. You can also substitute pears in the fall or winter.

APPLESAUCE

3½ lb (1.75 kg) tart-sweet apples such as Golden Delicious or Pink Lady, peeled, quartered, cored, quarters cut crosswise into ¾-inch thick pieces

½ cup (5½ oz/170 g) maple syrup, preferably grade B

Two 1-by-3-inch (2.5-by-7.5-cm) strips lemon peel

½ teaspoon ground cinnamon

½ teaspoon pure vanilla extract

In a large heavy saucepan over medium-high heat, bring the apples, 1½ cups (12 fl oz/375 ml) water, the maple syrup, lemon peel, and cinnamon to a boil. Reduce the heat so that the mixture simmers, cover, and cook until a chunky applesauce forms, stirring and breaking up the apples occasionally, about 40 minutes. Remove from the heat and stir in the vanilla. Let cool slightly. Transfer to a covered container and refrigerate until well chilled, at least 4 hours and up to 3 days. Makes about 3 cups.

MAPLE-BERRY TOPPING

2 cups (½ lb/250 g) fresh blueberries

3 tablespoons pure maple syrup, preferably grade B

1 cup (¼ lb/125 g) *each* fresh raspberries and blackberries

In a saucepan over medium heat, combine 1 cup (4 oz/125 g) of the blueberries, the maple syrup, and ¼ cup (2 fl oz/60 ml) water and simmer until a thick syrup forms, stirring frequently, about 7 minutes. In a bowl, combine the remaining 1 cup blueberries, the raspberries, blackberries, and the warm blueberry mixture. Using a rubber spatula, toss gently to coat. Cover and refrigerate for up to 6 hours. Makes 3 cups (12 oz/375 g).

NOTE: To add strawberries, cut into quarters and substitute for an equal quantity of other berries. For a topping with a rosier hue, cook 1 cup raspberries instead of blueberries.

WHIPPED CREAM

1 cup (8 fl oz/250 ml) cold heavy cream

2 tablespoons granulated sugar

½ teaspoon pure vanilla extract

Using a mixer, beat the cream in a bowl until soft peaks form. Add the granulated sugar and vanilla and beat until incorporated. Makes 2 cups (16 fl oz/500 ml).

MAPLE YOGURT CREAM

1 cup (8 fl oz/250 ml) cold heavy cream

2½ tablespoons maple syrup, preferably Grade B

½ teaspoon pure vanilla extract

½ cup (4 oz/125 g) plain Greek yogurt

Using a mixer, beat the cream in a chilled bowl until soft peaks form. Add the maple syrup and the vanilla and beat just to combine. Fold in the yogurt. Cover and refrigerate for up to 4 hours before using. Makes about 2½ cups (20 fl oz/625 ml).

LEMON CURD & WHIPPED LEMON FROSTING

½ cup unsalted (4 oz/125 g) unsalted butter, cut into cubes

¾ cup (6 oz/185 g) granulated sugar

¾ cup (6 fl oz/180 ml) fresh lemon juice

1½ tablespoons grated lemon zest

4 large eggs

1 large egg yolk

1 cup (8 fl oz/250 ml) cold heavy cream

½ cup (2 oz/60 g) confectioners' sugar

To make the lemon curd, set a fine-mesh sieve over a bowl. In a heavy saucepan over medium-high heat, combine the butter, granulated sugar, lemon juice, and lemon zest, and cook, stirring, until the sugar dissolves and the mixture just comes to a simmer. In another bowl, whisk together the eggs and egg yolk. Slowly add the hot lemon mixture to the eggs, whisking constantly. Pour the lemon-egg mixture back into the same saucepan and cook over medium-low heat, stirring constantly, until the curd thickens (do not boil), about 2 minutes. Immediately pour the curd into the sieve, pushing the curd through with a rubber spatula. Let cool slightly in the bowl. Cover with plastic wrap, pressing it directly onto the surface of the curd to prevent a skin from forming. Refrigerate until chilled, at least 6 hours and preferably overnight. Just before you are ready to frost the cake, transfer ⅔ cup (6 oz/170 g) of the cold curd to a bowl and set aside to spread on each cake layer before frosting.

To make the Whipped Lemon Frosting, using an electric mixer, beat the cream and confectioners' sugar in a bowl until soft peaks form. Fold one-third of the whipped cream into the remaining lemon curd to lighten it, and then fold in the remaining whipped cream just until incorporated. Makes about 2 cups (16 fl oz/500 ml).

NOTE: After frosting and refrigerating, if the frosting slumps slightly on the sides of the cake, use a rubber spatula to spread it back up the sides of the cake.

YOGURT–MEYER LEMON CURD

6 tablespoons (3 oz/90 g) unsalted butter, cut into pieces

½ cup (4 oz/125 g) sugar

½ cup (4 fl oz/125 ml) fresh Meyer lemon or lemon juice

1 tablespoon grated Meyer lemon zest or lemon zest

3 large eggs

½ cup (4 oz/125 g) plus 2 tablespoons plain Greek yogurt or ⅓ cup (3 fl oz/80 ml) cold heavy cream

Set a fine-mesh sieve over a bowl. In a heavy saucepan over medium heat, combine the butter, sugar, the lemon juice, and lemon zest, and cook, stirring until the sugar dissolves and the mixture just comes to a simmer. In another bowl, whisk together the eggs. Slowly add the hot lemon mixture to the eggs, whisking constantly. Pour the lemon-egg mixture back into the same saucepan and cook over medium-low heat, stirring constantly, until the curd thickens (do not boil), about 2 minutes. Immediately pour the curd into the sieve, pushing the curd through with a rubber spatula. Let cool slightly in the bowl. Cover with plastic wrap, pressing it directly onto the surface of the curd to prevent a skin from forming. Refrigerate until chilled, at least 4 hours.

If using Greek yogurt, fold it into the lemon curd. If using heavy cream, using an electric mixer, beat the cream in a bowl until stiff peaks form. Fold the cream into the curd. Cover and refrigerate for up to 4 hours. Makes about 2 cups (16 fl oz/500 ml).

GINGER-COCONUT CRUST

1 cup (3 oz/90 g) unsweetened shredded coconut, toasted and cooled

4 oz (125 g) gluten-free gingersnaps

2 tablespoons firmly packed brown sugar

Pinch of kosher salt

¼ cup (2 oz/60 g) unsalted butter, melted and cooled slightly

Preheat the oven to 375°F (190°C). In a food processor, pulse the toasted coconut, gingersnaps, brown sugar, and salt until the mixture is finely ground. Add the melted butter and process until moist clumps form. Scrape the crumb mixture into a 9-inch (23-cm) glass pie dish and press it evenly into the pan bottom and sides. Crimp the edges, if desired. Bake until the edges begin to

brown, about 8 minutes. Transfer the crust to a wire rack. If the crust is puffed in the center, us a small rubber spatula to gently press it down. Let cool completely.

NOTES: The crust can be made with pecans rather than coconut, or leave out the nuts and use 8 oz (250 g) of cookies.

CHOCOLATE TARTLET DOUGH

4½ oz (140 g) chopped semisweet or bittersweet chocolate

3 tablespoons oil

3 tablespoons honey

1¾ cups (7¼ oz/215 g) plus 2 tablespoons almond meal

¾ teaspoon ground cinnamon

Scant ½ teaspoon baking soda

¼ teaspoon coarse kosher salt

Place the chocolate in the top of a double boiler over barely simmering water. Heat, stirring often, until melted and smooth. Remove from over the water and stir in the oil and honey. In a bowl, whisk together the almond meal, cinnamon, baking soda, and salt. Pour the chocolate mixture into the dry ingredients and stir until smooth. Using a rubber spatula, divide the crust mixture evenly among six 4-inch (10-cm) tartlet pans and, using slightly damp hands, press evenly into the bottom and sides. Refrigerate until the crusts are firm, at least 20 minutes and up to overnight.

BASIC PIE & TART CRUST

½ cup (3¾ oz/110 g) brown rice flour

½ cup (1¾ oz/55 g) sorghum flour

⅓ cup (1¼ oz/35 g) tapioca flour

1½ tablespoons granulated sugar

⅜ teaspoon xanthan gum

Scant ¼ teaspoon kosher salt

½ cup (4 oz/125 g) cold unsalted butter, cut into ½-inch (12-mm) pieces

1 large egg, beaten

Cold water as needed

In a food processor, pulse the rice flour, sorghum flour, tapioca flour, sugar, xanthan gum, and salt to mix well. Add the butter and pulse until pea-sized lumps form. Add the egg and pulse until blended. If necessary, add the cold water, 1 tablespoon at a time, pulsing just until the dough forms a ball, scraping down the sides of the bowl as needed. Scrape the dough onto a sheet of waxed paper. Shape the dough into a ball and then flatten into a disk that's about ½ inch (12 mm) thick. Cover tightly with the waxed paper and refrigerate until firm, at least 1 hour and up to 1 day.

Dust the dough on both sides with sorghum flour and place between 2 large sheets of waxed paper on a work surface. Roll out the dough through the paper into a 12-inch (30-cm) round, removing the top sheet of paper and turning the dough over occasionally. Remove the top sheet of paper and, using the second sheet of paper, invert the dough into a 9-inch (23-cm) glass pie dish. Gently remove the paper. Using your fingers, press the dough into the dish bottom and sides. Fold over the excess dough on the edges. Using fingertips, crimp the crust all around the edge.

index

A

Almonds
  Almond-Ginger Crisps, 45
  almond meal, about, 10
  Almond-Oat Lace Cookies, 47
  Almond–Sour Cherry Muffins, 22
  Caramel-Nut Tartlets, 71
  Lemon Curd Almond Cake, 56
  Pine Nut & Almond Cookies, 44
Apples
  Apple-Cranberry Crumble, 97
  Apple Crumble Pie, 76
  Applesauce, 124
  Maple-Apple Trifles, 100

B

Banana Chocolate Bread, 120
Basic Corn Bread, 114
Berry-Peach-Cornmeal Crisp, 98
Blackberries
  Berry-Peach-Cornmeal Crisp, 98
  Blackberry-Cornmeal Cake, 60
  Gingerbread Blackberry Muffins, 24
  Maple-Berry Pavlova, 101
  Maple-Berry Topping, 124
Blueberries
  Cheesecake with Blueberry Sauce, 54
  Lemon-Berry Meringue Nests, 103
  Lemon-Blueberry Scones, 28
  Maple-Berry Pavlova, 101
  Maple-Berry Topping, 124
  Wild Blueberry Sauce, 124
Breads. *See also* Muffins; Scones
  Basic Corn Bread, 114
  Chile-Cheese Corn Bread, 115
  Chocolate Banana Bread, 120
  Crusty Millet Loaf, 121
  Olive & Sage Flatbread, 117
  Pumpkin-Date-Walnut Bread, 118
  Seeded Irish Soda Bread, 110
  Whole Grain–Walnut Bread, 113
Broccoli & Goat Cheese Quiche, 73
Brownies, Chocolate Walnut, 40
Buckwheat flour, about, 9
Buckwheat-Rosemary Scones, 27

C

Cakes
  Blackberry-Cornmeal Cake, 60
  Cheesecake with Blueberry Sauce, 54
  Chocolate-Cherry Torte, 59
  Cinnamon Crumb Cake, 18
  Gingerbread & Sautéed Peaches, 63
  Lemon Curd Almond Cake, 56
  Pumpkin-Spice Cheesecake, 61
Caramel-Nut Tartlets, 71
Chai-Spiced Flan, 88
Cheese
  Broccoli & Goat Cheese Quiche, 73
  Cheesecake with Blueberry Sauce, 54
  Chile-Cheese Corn Bread, 115
  Pumpkin-Spice Cheesecake, 61
  Sweet Pepper & Manchego Quiche, 75
Cherries
  Almond–Sour Cherry Muffins, 22
  Chocolate-Cherry Torte, 59
Chile-Cheese Corn Bread, 115
Chocolate
  Chocolate Banana Bread, 120
  Chocolate-Cherry Torte, 59
  Chocolate Chip–Ginger Scones, 29
  Chocolate Chip Meringues, 39
  Chocolate Chip Oatmeal Cookies, 37
  Chocolate-Tartlet Dough, 125
  Chocolate Walnut Brownies, 40
  Cinnamon-Chocolate Meringues, 41
  Fudgy Ginger-Nut Meringues, 34
  Meringue Ice Cream Sandwiches, 104
Cinnamon Crumb Cake, 18
Clafoutis, Pear, 83
Coconut
  Coconut-Lime Cream Pie, 68
  Coconut Macaroons, 43
  Ginger-Coconut Crust, 125
  Meringue Ice Cream Sandwiches, 104
Cookies & bars
  Almond-Ginger Crisps, 45
  Almond-Oat Lace Cookies, 47
  Chocolate Chip Oatmeal Cookies, 37
  Chocolate Walnut Brownies, 40
  Chocolate Chip Meringues, 39
  Coconut Macaroons, 43
  Fudgy Ginger-Nut Meringues, 34
  Pecan Thumbprint Cookies, 48
  Pine Nut & Almond Cookies, 44
  Vanilla Spice Meringues, 38

Cornmeal, 10
  Basic Corn Bread, 114
  Berry-Peach-Cornmeal Crisp, 97
  Blackberry-Cornmeal Cake, 60
  Chile-Cheese Corn Bread, 115
  Cornmeal-Pecan Muffins, 23
  Indian Pudding, 86
  Olive & Sage Flatbread, 117
Cornstarch, about, 9
Cranberries
  Apple-Cranberry Crumble, 97
  Maple-Orange Rice Pudding, 89
Crisp, Berry-Peach-Cornmeal, 98
Crumble, Apple-Cranberry, 97

D

Dairy products, 11
Date-Pumpkin-Walnut Bread, 118

E

Egg whites, working with, 12

F

Flaxseed meal, 10
  Seeded Irish Soda Bread, 110
  Whole Grain–Walnut Bread, 113

G

Ginger
  Almond-Ginger Crisps, 45
  Chocolate Chip–Ginger Scones, 29
  Fudgy Ginger-Nut Meringues, 34
  Gingerbread Blackberry Muffins, 24
  Gingerbread & Sautéed Peaches, 63
  Ginger-Coconut Crust, 125
  Vanilla-Ginger Crème Brûlée, 91
Gluten-free baking
  flours, 9–10, 11
  grains, 10–11
  pantry staples, 122–23
  starches, 9
  tips and tricks, 12

H

Hazelnuts
  Caramel-Nut Tartlets, 71
  Cheesecake with Blueberry Sauce, 54
  Fudgy Ginger-Nut Meringues, 34

I

Ice Cream Sandwiches, Meringue, 104
Indian Pudding, 86

L

Lemons
  Lemon-Berry Meringue Nests, 103
  Lemon-Blueberry Scones, 28
  Lemon Curd Almond Cake, 56
  Lemon Curd & Whipped Lemon Frosting,
    124–25
  Yogurt–Meyer Lemon Curd, 125
Lime-Coconut Cream Pie, 68

M

Macaroons, Coconut, 43
Maple-Apple Trifles, 100
Maple-Berry Pavlova, 101
Maple-Berry Topping, 124
Maple-Orange Rice Pudding, 87
Maple Yogurt Cream, 124
Meringue
  Chocolate Chip Meringues, 39
  Fudgy Ginger-Nut Meringues, 34
  Lemon-Berry Meringue Nests, 103
  Maple-Berry Pavlova, 101
  Meringue Ice Cream Sandwiches, 104
  Vanilla Spice Meringues, 38
Millet flour, about, 9
Millet Loaf, Crusty, 121
Muffins
  Almond–Sour Cherry Muffins, 22
  Cornmeal–Pecan Muffins, 23
  Gingerbread Blackberry Muffins, 24
  Raspberry Oatmeal Muffins, 21

O

Oats, 10
  Almond-Oat Lace Cookies, 47
  Chocolate Chip Oatmeal Cookies, 37
  Maple-Apple Trifles, 100
  oat bran, about, 11
  oat flour, about, 9
  Raspberry Oatmeal Muffins, 21
Oils, for baking, 11
Olive & Sage Flatbread, 117

P

Pavlova, Maple-Berry, 101

Peaches
  Berry-Peach-Cornmeal Crisp, 98
  Gingerbread & Sautéed Peaches, 63
  Sautéed Peaches, 124
Pear Clafoutis, 83
Pecans
  Cornmeal–Pecan Muffins, 23
  Pumpkin Gingersnap Pie, 72
  Pecan Thumbprint Cookies, 48
  Pumpkin-Spice Cheesecake, 61
Peppers
  Chile-Cheese Corn Bread, 115
  Sweet Pepper & Manchego Quiche, 75
Pies & tarts. See also Quiche
  Apple Crumble Pie, 76
  Caramel-Nut Tartlets, 71
  Coconut-Lime Cream Pie, 68
  Pumpkin Gingersnap Pie, 72
Pie & tart crusts
  Basic Pie & Tart Crust, 125
  Chocolate-Tartlet Dough, 125
  Ginger-Coconut Crust, 125
Pine Nut & Almond Cookies, 44
Potato starch, about, 9
Puddings & custards
  Chai-Spiced Flan, 88
  Indian Pudding, 86
  Maple-Orange Rice Pudding, 87
  Pear Clafoutis, 83
  Salted Caramel Pots de Crème, 84
  Vanilla-Ginger Crème Brûlée, 91
Pumpkin
  Pumpkin Gingersnap Pie, 72
  Pumpkin-Date-Walnut Bread, 118
  Pumpkin-Spice Cheesecake, 61

Q

Quiche
  Broccoli & Goat Cheese Quiche, 73
  Sweet Pepper & Manchego Quiche, 75
Quinoa flakes, about, 11
Quinoa flour, about, 9

R

Raspberries
  Maple-Berry Pavlova, 101
  Maple-Berry Topping, 124
  Raspberry Oatmeal Muffins, 21
Rice flour, about, 9–10

Rice Pudding, Maple-Orange, 89
Rosemary-Buckwheat Scones, 27

S

Salted Caramel Pots de Crème, 84
Sauces
  Applesauce, 124
  Maple-Berry Topping, 124
  Wild Blueberry Sauce, 124
Scones
  Chocolate Chip–Ginger Scones, 29
  Lemon-Blueberry Scones, 28
  Rosemary-Buckwheat Scones, 27
Seeded Irish Soda Bread, 110
Sorghum flour, about, 10
Strawberries
  Lemon-Berry Meringue Nests, 103

T

Tapioca flour, about, 10
Tartlets, Caramel-Nut, 71
Trifles, Maple-Apple, 100

V

Vanilla-Ginger Crème Brûlée, 91
Vanilla Spice Meringues, 38

W

Walnuts
  Apple-Cranberry Crumble, 97
  Caramel-Nut Tartlets, 71
  Chocolate Walnut Brownies, 40
  Cinnamon Crumb Cake, 18
  Gingerbread & Sautéed Peaches, 63
  Pumpkin-Date-Walnut Bread, 118
  Whole Grain–Walnut Bread, 113
Whipped Cream, 124
Whole Grain–Walnut Bread, 113
Wild Blueberry Sauce, 124

X

Xanthan gum, about, 11

Y

Yogurt
  Maple Yogurt Cream, 124
  Yogurt–Meyer Lemon Curd, 125

weldon**owen**

415 Jackson Street, 3rd Floor, San Francisco, CA 94111
www.weldonowen.com

GLUTEN-FREE BAKING

Conceived and produced by Weldon Owen, Inc.
In collaboration with Williams-Sonoma, Inc.
3250 Van Ness Avenue, San Francisco, CA 94109

A WELDON OWEN PRODUCTION

Copyright © 2014 Weldon Owen, Inc.
and Williams-Sonoma, Inc.

All rights reserved, including the right of
reproduction in whole or in part in any form.

Printed and bound in China by 1010 Printing, Ltd.

First printed in 2014
10 9 8 7 6 5 4 3 2

Library of Congress Control Number: 2014943527

ISBN 13: 978-1-61628-810-5
ISBN 10: 1-61628-810-8

Weldon Owen is a division of
BONNIER

WELDON OWEN, INC

CEO and President Terry Newell
VP, Sales and Marketing Amy Kaneko
VP, Publisher Roger Shaw
Finance Director Philip Paulick

Associate Publisher Jennifer Newens
Associate Editor Emma Rudolph

Creative Director Kelly Booth
Art Director Alisha Petro
Senior Production Designer Rachel Lopez Metzger

Production Director Chris Hemesath
Associate Production Director Michelle Duggan

Photographer Annabelle Breakey
Food Stylist Jeffrey Larsen
Food Stylist Assistant Abby Stolfo
Prop Stylist Ethel Brennan

ACKNOWLEDGEMENTS

Weldon Owen wishes to thank the following people for their
generous support in producing this book: Carole Bidnick, Jane Tunks Demel,
Jackie Hancock, Amy Hatwig, Kim Laidlaw, Amy Marr, and Hilary Seeley